READINGS ON

NATHANIEL HAWTHORNE

THE GREENHAVEN PRESS
Literary Companion
TO AMERICAN AUTHORS

NATHANIEL HAWTHORNE

David Bender, *Publisher*
Bruno Leone, *Executive Editor*
Scott Barbour, *Managing Editor*
Clarice Swisher, *Book Editor*

Greenhaven Press, San Diego, CA

Library of Congress Cataloging-in-Publication Data

Readings on Nathaniel Hawthorne / Clarice Swisher, book
    editor.
        p.   cm. — (Greenhaven Press literary companion to
        American authors)
    Includes bibliographical references (p.   ) and index.
    ISBN 1-56510-459-5 (lib. : alk. paper). —
ISBN 1-56510-458-7 (pbk. : alk. paper)
    1. Hawthorne, Nathaniel, 1804–1864—Criticism and
interpretation. I. Swisher, Clarice, 1933–   . II. Series
PS1888.R43   1996
813'.3–dc20   95-43122
                                                                CIP

Cover photo: The Bettmann Archive

Copyright ©1996 by Greenhaven Press, Inc.
PO Box 289009
San Diego, CA 92198-9009
Printed in the U.S.A.

I do not want to be a doctor and live by men's diseases, nor a minister to live by their sins, nor a lawyer and live by their quarrels. So, I don't see that there is anything left for me but to be an author.

—Nathaniel Hawthorne, at seventeen

CONTENTS

Nathaniel Hawthorne, quiet and thoughtful by nature, found subject matter for stories in his native New England. He roamed the region's farms, docks, markets, and taverns observing local citizens and listening to their tales. Using his imagination to enhance these experiences, he wrote stories of fantasy and morality, many of which make creative use of symbols.

Nathaniel Hawthorne expressed uncertainty about his worth as a writer even after his early tales had succeeded with readers. This self-doubt resulted from the influence of two of his uncles. His uncle Samuel Manning fostered Hawthorne's artistic tendency. His uncle Robert Manning instilled in Hawthorne doubt about the legitimacy of fiction writing as a profession. These two conflicting forces drive the action of "The Story Teller" sequence.

Forced by family circumstances to spend his childhood alone, Nathaniel Hawthorne learned the value of solitude. He reflected on his Puritan ancestry and practiced his writing skills for more than a decade in Salem, Massachusetts. He emerged from this quiet period with tales and a novel, *The Scarlet Letter*, that reveal the mind of New England Puritanism. The naturalness of his art—his deeply human Puritan characters and his fidelity to no style but his own—distinguishes Hawthorne as an important nineteenth-century writer.

Nathaniel Hawthorne deliberately chose to study writing and Puritanism, tasks that he could only do alone. Otherwise, he was a public person, living with and observing his fellow New Englanders or performing his duties as a foreign consul. Hawthorne's interest in the lives of his fellow humans led him to examine the relationship between the individual and society. Guilt, he concluded, corroded lives, while nature and the freedom from guilt brought "sweetness."

Early in Nathaniel Hawthorne's career, publishers and

reviewers enthusiastically predicted his success. Fellow writers Edgar Allan Poe and Herman Melville promoted his reputation and referred to his qualities of genius. Yet, Hawthorne, who liked to hike, feared that only the path he trod would remember him, according to the 1865 journal of Ralph Waldo Emerson. After Hawthorne's death in 1864, British writer Matthew Arnold said of Hawthorne that "his literary talent is of the first order." In 1949 scholars of American literature ranked him in first place among American authors.

Nathaniel Hawthorne belonged neither to the new industrialism of his time nor to the Puritan past. He viewed the new machine age with indifference, and he regarded the hope and optimism of transcendentalists with skepticism. Already he had rejected the Calvinist religious doctrine of his ancestors. Skeptical of both the present and the past, Hawthorne chose the subject of Puritan rigidity in which to explore the psychological effects of sin. His characters are failures, victims, and deluded people caught up in wrongdoing. Hawthorne developed themes around the effect of sin on their minds and spirits.

Nathaniel Hawthorne's *Mosses from an Old Manse* reveals the dark, mystical blackness of Hawthorne's vision. This blackness is much like that expressed by William Shakespeare, whose tragic characters express dark truths. The blackness is not a symbol for sin or evil in either author's work. Rather, it represents a quality more complex, more deeply lodged within the human psyche, and gives expression to the negative emotions—the anguish and despair—that humans are capable of experiencing.

Two previously overlooked children's books provide insight into Nathaniel Hawthorne's use of mythological themes to construct his own personal myth. Expressed through symbols and allegories, the myth is present in all of his tales and novels. At the center of the myth is the heart, which is divided between reason and imagination. Like heroes in Greek stories, Hawthorne's characters pursue a hero's quest, but they can succeed only if they reconcile the opposites of reason and imagination.

At the beginning of his career, Nathaniel Hawthorne needed to find a voice, an attitude, and a setting, in order to express his spiritual insights. He joined the transcendentalists in their experiment in communal living on Brook Farm, but he found neither the idealistic transcendentalists nor com-

munal living compatible with his spirit. As a romantic, he
wanted to look to the past, but America had but a short and
thin history. For a time he lived in Rome, a city whose long
history had shadows and mysteries. In the end, however,
he found that his own Puritan ancestors provided him
with abundant material to give voice to tales and novels
that explore the human condition.

Nathaniel Hawthorne struggled with two questions: Should
he portray the imaginative or actual world? and, Should he
use symbolism or allegory? Hawthorne never resolved these
dilemmas entirely. In *The Scarlet Letter*, Hawthorne writes as
a symbolist. In *The Marble Faun* and *The Blithedale
Romance*, however, Hawthorne is neither a successful symbolist nor an effective allegorist. These unresolved issues
weaken the novels.

Nathaniel Hawthorne's romantic characters and themes
developed in stages. Like other romantic writers, Hawthorne
wrote about guilt, alienation, and the past. In Hawthorne's
works, a guilty character develops self-identity while alienated from society. The character accepts alienation, exploits
society's guilt, and finds empathy in connection with others.
When the character is ready to reenter society, he or she is
also ready for redemption. Hawthorne handled most of these
romantic problems easily, but he never mastered the theme
of social redemption, wherein the romantic individual transforms society.

Nathaniel Hawthorne created three kinds of female characters from real-life women he knew and from characters in
his earlier works. There are wholesome New England girls,
such as Phoebe in *The House of the Seven Gables*. His graceful creatures, such as Priscilla in *The Blithedale Romance*,
are more delicate. Finally, Hawthorne creates rich, exotic
women, such as Hester in *The Scarlet Letter*. Hawthorne saw
qualities in his wife Sophia that he attributed to all three
kinds of women.

Twice-Told Tales brings together stories for entertainment
and stories with symbolic meaning. Nathaniel Hawthorne
had written sketches and tales for gift books, which were
popular among moral, genteel ladies who liked sentimental
stories. He had also written serious stories in which he
explored multiple meanings and invented symbols. *Twice-
Told Tales* blends these two kinds of stories, which, when

taken together, make a whole that "is surely greater than the sum of its parts."

FOREWORD

*"'Tis the good reader that
makes the good book."*

Ralph Waldo Emerson

The story's bare facts are simple: The captain, an old and scarred seafarer, walks with a peg leg made of whale ivory. He relentlessly drives his crew to hunt the world's oceans for the great white whale that crippled him. After a long search, the ship encounters the whale and a fierce battle ensues. Finally the captain drives his harpoon into the whale, but the harpoon line catches the captain about the neck and drags him to his death.

A simple story, a straightforward plot—yet, since the 1851 publication of Herman Melville's *Moby-Dick*, readers and critics have found many meanings in the struggle between Captain Ahab and the whale. To some, the novel is a cautionary tale that depicts how Ahab's obsession with revenge leads to his insanity and death. Others believe that the whale represents the unknowable secrets of the universe and that Ahab is a tragic hero who dares to challenge fate by attempting to discover this knowledge. Perhaps Melville intended Ahab as a criticism of Americans' tendency to become involved in well-intentioned but irrational causes. Or did Melville model Ahab after himself, letting his fictional character express his anger at what he perceived as a cruel and distant god?

Although literary critics disagree over the meaning of *Moby-Dick*, readers do not need to choose one particular interpretation in order to gain an understanding of Melville's novel. Instead, by examining various analyses, they can gain numerous insights into the issues that lie under the surface of the basic plot. Studying the writings of literary critics can also aid readers in making their own assessments of *Moby-Dick* and other literary works and in developing analytical thinking skills.

The Greenhaven Literary Companion Series was created with these goals in mind. Designed for young adults, this unique anthology series provides an engaging and comprehensive introduction to literary analysis and criticism. The essays included in the Literary Companion Series are chosen for their accessibility to a young adult audience and are expertly edited in consideration of both the reading and comprehension levels of this audience. In addition, each essay is introduced by a concise summation that presents the contributing writer's main themes and insights. Every anthology in the Literary Companion Series contains a varied selection of critical essays that cover a wide time span and express diverse views. Wherever possible, primary sources are represented through excerpts from authors' notebooks, letters, and journals and through contemporary criticism.

Each title in the Literary Companion Series pays careful consideration to the historical context of the particular author or literary work. In-depth biographies and detailed chronologies reveal important aspects of authors' lives and emphasize the historical events and social milieu that influenced their writings. To facilitate further research, every anthology includes primary and secondary source bibliographies of articles and/or books selected for their suitability for young adults. These engaging features make the Greenhaven Literary Companion Series ideal for introducing students to literary analysis in the classroom or as a library resource for young adults researching the world's great authors and literature.

Exceptional in its focus on young adults, the Greenhaven Literary Companion Series strives to present literary criticism in a compelling and accessible format. Every title in the series is intended to spark readers' interest in leading American and world authors, to help them broaden their understanding of literature, and to encourage them to formulate their own analyses of the literary works that they read. It is the editors' hope that young adult readers will find these anthologies to be true companions in their study of literature.

Nathaniel Hawthorne: A Biography

Biographers and critics of Nathaniel Hawthorne must deal with opposites—determination and self-doubt, imagery of light and dark, flowers and weeds—paradoxes, and ambiguity interwoven through Hawthorne's life and his works. Taken together, these conflicting elements permit a variety of interpretations. Hawthorne himself was preoccupied with the problems of evil, the nature of sin, the conflict between pride and humility, and the role of imagination in a materialistic society. But Hawthorne's interest tended toward the heart and the psychological effects of these moral and ethical issues.

Many biographers have looked to Hawthorne's formative years for insight into his work. Hawthorne descended from two families whose ancestry can be traced back to early colonial times. William Hathorne (Nathaniel added the "w" to the last name), who came to America in 1630, and Nicholas Manning, who came in 1660, both settled in Salem, Massachusetts. Both families strongly influenced young Nathaniel, but in different ways. The Hathornes influenced him indirectly from the remote past, the Mannings directly in the immediate present.

Nathaniel Hawthorne was born on the fourth of July 1804 in Salem, Massachusetts, the son of Captain Nathaniel and Elizabeth Hathorne. The couple had two other children: Elizabeth Manning, born in 1802, and Maria Louisa, born in 1808. Captain Hathorne had followed generations of Hathorne men into a career as a merchant seaman, a job that took him away from home for many months of the year. When Nathaniel was four years old, his father died of yellow fever on a voyage to the Caribbean. At the time, the twenty-eight-year-old Elizabeth and her three children were living with Captain Hathorne's parents. Shocked by the death of her husband and uncomfortable with her in-laws, Elizabeth Hathorne moved with her children to the home of her parents, the Mannings, and her eight brothers and sisters.

Influence of the Mannings and Hathornes

Life with the Mannings brought many changes in Nathaniel's life. Between the ages of four and nine, Nathaniel lived in a house with six Manning men. His grandfather, Richard Manning Sr., had been a blacksmith and later became a business-man who dealt in real estate and owned stagecoach lines. He and his wife, Miriam, had five sons—William, Richard, Robert, John, and Samuel—and four daughters—Mary, Elizabeth (Hawthorne's mother), Priscilla, and Maria Miriam. Elizabeth, a submissive woman mourning the loss of her husband, left her children's upbringing to her family. When Nathaniel's grandfather Richard died, his uncle Robert took over as head of the household and as Nathaniel's primary guardian. Robert exert-ed firm discipline to teach Nathaniel about the manly role of responsibility and the practical need to earn a living, and Mary Manning instilled in the boy a dedication to work and studies.

Despite their dedication to practical matters and their mate-rial interests, the Mannings had an artistic, creative side. Robert cultivated fruit groves; Richard liked books and wanted a harp; Priscilla wrote letters with artistic literary style; and Samuel, only twelve years older than Nathaniel, lived a life of freedom and fun. Young Nathaniel preferred the sensitive, cre-ative aspects of this environment and resented Robert's con-trolling manner, but the boy never revolted outwardly against the stern, practical discipline and assumed that he too would become a businessman. In *Family Themes and Hawthorne's Fiction: The Tenacious Web*, Gloria C. Erlich writes, "Nathaniel's passivity and indolence appeared especially unmanly in the presence of Robert Manning's energetic capabilities, not only to the uncle but to the boy himself. The resulting self-distrust was to be permanently in conflict with Hawthorne's innate pride." In 1820, Hawthorne wrote in a letter to his sister Elizabeth, "No man can be a Poet and a Bookkeeper at the same time."

The early Hathorne ancestors were of little significance to Nathaniel until, as a young adult, he learned about their roles in Puritan New England history. William Hathorne was a colo-nial magistrate involved in the persecution of Quakers, anoth-er Protestant religious group. Hawthorne later described him as "grave, bearded, sable-cloaked, and steeple-crowned," a hard, dark man. His son John Hathorne was well known as a Puritan judge who condemned women as witches in 1692 dur-ing the Salem witchcraft trials, and who later expressed no remorse for his actions. According to a family story, one of the so-called witches pronounced a curse on Judge Hathorne and all of his posterity. After the original father and son, the fol-lowing generations of Hathornes were known to history only in their roles as merchant sea captains. Of his ancestors, especially Judge John, Hawthorne later said, "I . . . hereby take shame upon myself for their sakes, and pray that any curse incurred by them . . . may be now and henceforth removed." But he also realized that these Puritan ancestors had influenced his own life, writing, "Strong traits of their nature have intertwined themselves with mine."

Both the stern, religious Hathornes of the past and the stern, business-minded Mannings of the present exerted a power on young Nathaniel that conflicted with his sensitive nature and his artistic interests. As a child, he read poetry, adventure and mystery stories, and colonial history. When he was nine, he injured his foot playing ball and was lame for three years. His lameness had subsided by 1816 when Elizabeth and her children moved to a Manning house on the shore of Lake Sebago in Raymond, Maine. Here Hawthorne loved roaming the woods and fishing on the lake. After three years of idyllic life in nature, the Mannings brought Nathaniel, now fifteen, back to Salem to attend the Samuel H. Archer School to prepare for college, even though Nathaniel wanted to stay in Maine. During this period he kept the books for the Manning stage-coach lines for a salary of one dollar a week, an income adequate for his wants. He continued to read; he now liked British poet Edmund Spenser's *The Faerie Queen,* John Bunyan's *Pilgrim's Progress,* and Shakespeare's plays. By age seventeen, he knew he wanted to be a writer: "I do not want to be a doctor and live by men's diseases, nor a minister to live by their sins, nor a lawyer and live by their quarrels. So, I don't see that there is anything left for me but to be an author."

HAWTHORNE'S COLLEGE YEARS

Hawthorne entered Bowdoin College in Brunswick, Maine, in 1821. Bowdoin was a small but highly regarded men's college with 114 students. To be admitted, he had to present a certificate of good moral character and pass an oral examination testing his knowledge of Latin grammar and classical Greek and Roman writers. While there, Hawthorne studied Latin, Greek, mathematics, philosophy, English composition, and natural science, but received little instruction in modern languages, modern literature, and history.

In addition to his classes, he joined one of the college's literary societies, which were study and social groups, similar, perhaps to early fraternities. Hawthorne enjoyed the social and the intellectual activities of college life and made lifelong friends of three literary society classmates—future poet Henry

Wadsworth Longfellow, future president Franklin Pierce, and future navy commodore Horatio Bridge.

Hawthorne was an average student, graduating eighteenth out of a class of thirty-eight in 1825. By that time, his mother and sisters had left Maine and moved into a house built for them next to Robert Manning's house in Salem. For the next twelve years, from 1825 to 1837, Hawthorne lived in this house preparing his mind and developing his skills. He still wanted to be a writer, the career he had chosen when he was seventeen. He wanted to be a writer of quality, and in order to accomplish this, he felt that he needed to think and reflect, to read widely, and to practice the craft of writing. His mother's house was the ideal place to do this work because it had quiet rooms in which he could be alone without interruption.

HAWTHORNE'S SOLITUDE IN SALEM

Throughout this period, Hawthorne spent mornings and afternoons writing and evenings reading. Records show that he borrowed some twelve hundred works of nonfiction from the library of the Salem Athenaeum. But he also read tales and novels and made studies of them. His sister Elizabeth, also a great reader, was regularly involved in selecting books and often read the same ones that Hawthorne read. During this period, he also studied his Puritan past. He read histories of the New England Puritan colony, diaries kept by leaders and ordinary colonists, sermons, accounts of the witchcraft trials, and the religious philosophies of the early Puritan leaders. Familiar colonial writers were among his readings: William Bradford, John Winthrop, and Cotton and Increase Mather. But Hawthorne did more than gather knowledge: He reflected and daydreamed and thought until he had absorbed the way of life and mind of his distant Hathorne relatives.

Though reading was an important activity during his twelve years in his mother's house, Hawthorne spent more of his time writing. He practiced writing historical sketches and allegorical tales. When he could find no publisher for his first collection of tales, he tossed them into the fire. In 1828, he published a novel, *Fanshawe*, anonymously, at his own expense, but critics and reviewers paid it no attention. Soon after its publication, Hawthorne came to dislike the novel, suppressed its distribution, and convinced his friend Horatio Bridge to destroy his copy. Today, ironically, it is one of the rarest and most valuable titles in American literature.

One tale that survived the fire, "The Hollow of Three Hills," was first published in the *Salem Gazette* in 1830. But when his second set of tales was ready for publication, again Hawthorne could find no one to publish them as a collection. He sent them to Samuel G. Goodrich, the editor of *Token*, an annual gift book, but Goodrich was interested only in individual stories. Goodrich published one story in 1831, and in 1832 he published "The Gentle Boy" (for which he paid Hawthorne thirty-five dollars) and three others. He published two more in 1833, three in 1835, three in 1836, and nine in 1837. All of these stories were published anonymously or under various pseudonyms. The editors of the *New England Magazine* published eight stories anonymously in 1835. Though he was getting his work published Hawthorne complained to Horatio Bridge in 1836 that he could earn no more than three hundred dollars a year by writing stories for magazines and annual gift books. A third collection of tales organized as a collection, *The Story Teller*, had also failed to win acceptance from a publisher. To supplement his income, Hawthorne worked for a short time as a magazine editor; he spent six months editing the *American Magazine of Useful and Entertaining Knowledge*, but he felt the work interfered with his own writing.

Hawthorne clearly needed a higher income than he was earning by selling individual stories. Horatio Bridge persuaded him to prepare a collection of his best tales and publish them under his own name. Hawthorne selected eighteen previously published stories, gave them the title *Twice-Told Tales*, and submitted them to Goodrich. Without Hawthorne's knowledge, Bridge guaranteed Goodrich $250 against losses. *Twice-Told Tales* was published in March 1837, and its immediate success, though modest, encouraged the author. The collection received two favorable reviews and a third glowing review by Henry Wadsworth Longfellow, his college friend, to whom Hawthorne had sent a complimentary copy.

TRAVELS BY FOOT AND STAGE

Though Hawthorne worked diligently at his vocation—reading, writing, and reflecting—he was not always cloistered in his room. He often visited his family, and he attended community gatherings, such as the visit of President Andrew Jackson to Salem. He continued to go on walks as a form of recreation, recording in notebooks his hikes to North Salem, to the shore, and along the railroad tracks. He and Horatio Bridge kept in touch through letters, and Hawthorne visited Bridge periodically in Augusta, Maine. Perhaps his most artistically fruitful recreation was the summer trips he took with his uncle Samuel Manning, who traveled around New England buying horses for the Manning stagecoach lines. Hawthorne's notebooks record descriptions of several excursions to, for example, New Haven, Connecticut, the Shaker community in New Hampshire, and Burlington, Vermont. On these summer journeys, Hawthorne says, he experienced "as much of life as other people do in the whole year round." In particular, his detailed observations of women encountered in his travels form the basis for women characters that appear in his later works.

Hawthorne's twelve "solitary" years were of mixed benefit. He came to the conclusion that he could never earn enough money writing for magazines to live comfortably. He would have to look to other sources for income. Having focused so exclusively on writing, however, he felt cut off from the activities of ordinary working people. In a letter to Longfellow, he wrote, "I have been carried apart from the main current of life. . . . I have made a captive of myself and put me into a dungeon, and now I cannot find the key to let me out—and if the door were open, I should be almost afraid to come out." But he had read much and written a great deal. He had mastered the writer's craft, gained knowledge of human nature, and gathered impressions which he could incorporate into his future tales and romances.

When Hawthorne called his stories "romances," he meant that they belong within the romantic movement that developed in Europe and America influencing the arts of painting, music, and literature. Romanticism developed as an alternative to reason and society's restrictions on the individual. Although it lacks rigid rules and specific boundaries, romanticism has recognizable elements. Romantic stories emphasize imagination and personal freedom. With an attitude of idealism and heroic struggle, romanticists often glorify nature, portray the mystery of the past and of remote places, and express optimism about the individual struggling on the frontier. Hawthorne's years of study put him in touch with romantic writers and allowed him to clarify his place among them.

INTO THE WORLD BEYOND SALEM

What had been for Hawthorne an apprenticeship in writing came to an end, and he left his "dungeon" in 1838. After spending a month with Bridge in Maine, he visited North Adams, Massachusetts. In his journal—a kind of artist's sketchbook—he recorded twenty-five thousand words describing people and places in detail. His story "Ethan Brand" contains characters like the people he described in this journal.

Late in 1838, he met Sophia Peabody, daughter of Dr. Nathaniel Peabody, a Salem dentist who later moved to Boston. Though Sophia was sickly with chronic nervous headaches, she was a beautiful woman of taste, well educated and accomplished. She read Latin, Greek, and Hebrew, and had talent in drawing, painting, and sculpture. At the end of 1838, she drew a sketch of Ilbrahim, the child in "The Gentle Boy," that was included with a new edition of the story. By the end of the year, Nathaniel and Sophia were in love and secretly became engaged.

In March 1839, at an annual salary of fifteen hundred dollars per year, Hawthorne obtained a political appointment from Democrats to the Boston Custom House, where he became a weigher and gauger of salt and coal. Separated from Sophia and deeply in love, he spent his evenings writing letters to her. These describe routine tasks at his work, often with humor, as well as expressions of his feelings for Sophia. In one he writes:

> Thou hast taught me that I have a heart. . . . Indeed, we are but shadows till the heart is touched. . . . Thou keepest my heart pure, and elevatest me above the world. Thou enablest me to interpret the riddle of life, and fillest me with faith in the unseen and better land, because thou leadest me thither continually. . . . It is a miracle worthy even of thee to have converted a life of shadows into the deepest truth by thy magic touch. . . . God gave you to me to be the salvation of my soul.

Sophia, as much in love as Nathaniel, returned his expressions of devotion in love letters to him. Hawthorne continued in his job at the customhouse until he resigned in January 1841.

Hawthorne's resignation corresponded to the time when a group of New Englanders were formulating plans for an experiment in utopian living. Brook Farm, an economic experiment in simple living, began in 1841 as a stock company called Brook Farm Institute of Agriculture and Education in West Roxbury, Massachusetts, nine miles from Boston. Its purpose was to promote culture and brotherly cooperation and obtain for its members the highest possible benefits of physical, intellectual, and moral education. Members, who joined of their own free will, all received the same benefits and the same pay for their work. The experiment was particularly popular with writers and philosophers who agreed with transcendentalist ideas. In 1843, Brook Farm came under the influence of people who followed the ideals of French socialist writer

Charles Fourier. The Brook Farm project folded in 1847.

In April 1841, Hawthorne invested a thousand dollars and joined Brook Farm, where he worked enthusiastically at tending animals and farming crops. By August, he questioned its plan, could see that it was not a financial success, and was tired of the hard work. After a visit to Salem, he returned briefly as a boarder, but he found too much disruption for his writing and left in November. He wrote, "It is my opinion that a man's soul may be buried under a dung heap or in a furrow of the field just as well as under a pile of money."

MARRIAGE AND OLD MANSE

After a three-year engagement, Hawthorne lost patience waiting to marry Sophia until he had more money. On July 7, 1842, Nathaniel Hawthorne and Sophia Peabody were married at the home of Sophia's parents in Boston. The couple then rented Old Manse, Ralph Waldo Emerson's ancestral home in Concord, just a few miles from Boston.

The Hawthornes spent four happy years at Old Manse. Though they had an active social life, they called their time there "a solitude for two." Their first child, Una, a girl, was born there in March 1844. In *Family Themes and Hawthorne's Fiction: The Tenacious Web*, Gloria C. Erlich explains the success of Nathaniel and Sophia's marriage:

> The marriage was beneficial for both partners. It gave Hawthorne intimate human contact and links to normal human experience. It led Sophia from chronic invalidism into sufficient health for motherhood and a fairly long, active life. With it, both found a satisfying and enduring physical relationship that made their separations hard to endure.

Sophia's friend Margaret Fuller wrote to Sophia, "If ever I saw a man who combined delicate tenderness to understanding the heart of a woman, with quiet depth and manliness to satisfy her, it is Mr. Hawthorne."

As Concord was the home of many of the transcendentalists, the Hawthornes were in their midst at Old Manse. This suited Sophia, who was more sympathetic to their ideas than was Hawthorne. Subscribers to transcendentalism, a philosophic and literary movement that falls within the broader romantic movement, reacted against the rational philosophers from Europe, such as John Locke, and the restrictive religion of Calvinism. They believed that God is embodied in the natural world and that the individual can recognize God intuitively. Each individual, they believed, has a soul which reflects the mystical elements of the soul of the world. Emerson had expressed many of these ideas in his 1836 book *Nature*. Shortly after *Nature*'s publication, transcendentalists formed their own magazine, the *Dial*, which was edited by Margaret Fuller. Hawthorne, who had a vivid sense that life contains dark and gloomy realities, never subscribed entirely to transcendentalist thought.

Between 1838 and 1845, Hawthorne published twenty-two stories in the *Democratic Review*, which paid him between three and five dollars a page, and he published nine stories in various other literary magazines. Besides his journal descriptions, letters to Sophia, and many tales, he wrote several children's books. *Grandfather's Chair* (1841), a children's history of New England through the Revolutionary War, sold over a million copies, but Hawthorne received only a hundred dollars for the manuscript. He also wrote *Famous Old People* (1841), *Liberty Tree* (1841), and *Biographical Stories for Children* (1842). Also in 1842, he published a new enlarged edition of *Twice-Told Tales*. It was this edition that Edgar Allan Poe reviewed in *Graham's Magazine*, praising Hawthorne's style and imagination. In 1846, Hawthorne published *Mosses from an Old Manse*, a collection of twenty-three pieces. Seventeen of these pieces he wrote at Old Manse, four had been published separately before 1837, and two he had passed over when selecting pieces for *Twice-Told Tales*. In 1850, New England novelist Herman Melville discovered Hawthorne's *Mosses* and wrote a review praising Hawthorne's genius and identifying his dark meaning. Melville recognized that elements of gloom, guilt, evil, and mystery reside in the remote regions of Hawthorne's characters.

SALEM AGAIN AND THE CUSTOMHOUSE

The Hawthornes left Old Manse in 1845 and moved to Hawthorne's mother's house in Salem. In Salem, Hawthorne again needed to supplement his writing income. On April 3, 1846, President James Polk signed Hawthorne's appointment to a post at the customhouse at the port of Salem at a salary of twelve hundred dollars a year. By this time, Salem had lost much of its seaport activity to Boston, and Hawthorne was less busy than he was at the Boston Custom House. In June, a son, Julian, was born. Hawthorne and Sophia remained happy, and Hawthorne enjoyed his role as parent, trying to record his children's activities and their development. He said of parenthood, "When a man has taken upon himself to beget children, he has no longer any right to a life of his own." He did, however, find time to be the secretary of the Salem Lyceum, an organization that engaged informative speakers. Moreover, he also found time to keep in touch with his friends Bridge and Longfellow, and friends in the Democratic Party. Soon after Whig Zachary Taylor won the 1848 presidential election, however, Hawthorne lost his post at the customhouse. While he was still angry about losing his political appointment and worried about supporting a wife and two children, his mother became gravely ill. She died on July 31, 1849. From a long emotional account in his notebook, he wrote about a visit to his mother two days before she died:

> For a long time, I knelt there, holding her hand: and surely it is the darkest hour I ever lived. Afterwards, I stood by the open window, and looked through the crevice of the curtain. The shouts, laughter, and cries of the two children had come up into the chamber, from the open air, making a strange contrast with the death-bed scene.

But sadness and worry did not keep him from writing. By September 27, 1849, Hawthorne had begun working on a new book, a story based on an account and a worn capital *A* that he had discovered in an upstairs storage area in the customhouse. In the essay "The Custom House," which introduces *The Scarlet Letter*, Hawthorne describes his find:

> But the object that most drew my attention, in the mysterious package, was a certain affair of fine red cloth, much worn and faded. There were traces about it of gold embroidery, which, however, was greatly frayed and defaced; so that none, or very little, of the glitter was left. It had been wrought, as was easy to perceive, with wonderful skill of needlework. . . . This rag of scarlet cloth,—for time, and wear, and a sacrilegious moth, had reduced it to little other than a rag,—on careful examination, assumed the shape of a letter. It was the capital letter A.

With his imagination set alight by the faded *A*, Hawthorne worked on a story about it, sometimes nine hours a day, completing the whole book in six months. *The Scarlet Letter* was published in Boston on March 16, 1850, and in England soon after. It sold six thousand copies in America at seventy-five cents a copy, of which Hawthorne earned 10 percent, or $450. Most critics acclaimed the book, although a few found it gloomy and immoral. Most of the reviews praised the essay on the customhouse as a humorous account of local Salem, but town residents were outraged by Hawthorne's description of Salem as a declining seaport town.

With his literary reputation established and the Salem residents angry with him, Hawthorne moved in May 1850 to a farmhouse in Lenox, a village in western Massachusetts. He could now relax and enjoy gardening, building, fishing, and playing with his children. On August 5, he met Herman Melville, who lived nearby. When they met, Melville, younger by fifteen years, only knew Hawthorne from his reading of *Mosses from an Old Manse*, but the two authors found that they had much in common. Since Melville had a horse and Hawthorne did not, Melville often visited Hawthorne at the farmhouse. Randall Stewart identifies their common qualities in *Nathaniel Hawthorne: A Biography*:

> . . . an intellectual honesty and disinterestedness, a skepticism, a distrust of fashionable panaceas, a sense of the humor as well as the tragedy of life, and an appreciation also of life's good things. Both could be at once Olympian and down to earth.

It is possible that both men stimulated each other's imagination and influenced each other's creative work. In the fall of 1850, Melville began writing *Moby-Dick* and Hawthorne began *The House of the Seven Gables*. Melville dedicated *Moby-Dick*, which he completed in the fall of 1851, to Hawthorne.

The year and a half in Lenox was a productive writing time for Hawthorne. *The House of the Seven Gables*, completed in January 1851 and published in April, was received with greater enthusiasm in America than was *The Scarlet Letter*, and was even more popular in England. Shortly after completing *The House of the Seven Gables*, Hawthorne wrote *A Wonder-Book for Girls and Boys*, a children's book of tales adapted from Greek myths. To test its suitability for young people, he tried out the stories on Una and Julian. In addition, he wrote "Feathertop," a satirical story published in two installments in the *International Magazine*. He wrote a new preface and published the third edition of *Twice-Told Tales*. And he wrote a preface for *The Snow Image and Other Twice-Told Tales*, another collection of tales. This collection contained four stories written after *Mosses*, "The Snow Image," "The Great Stone Face," "Main Street," and "Ethan Brand." The other seven in this collection were those he had passed over when selecting stories for *Twice-Told Tales*.

In May 1851, the Hawthornes' third child, Rose, was born. Though he was earning more money than in previous years from the sale of books, Hawthorne's expenses were rising. By fall, he was tiring of Lenox and longing to be nearer the sea and the city streets. After a dispute with the owner of the farmhouse, Hawthorne left Lenox on November 21, 1851. Briefly, the family stayed with relatives until they found Wayside, a home on nine acres of land in Concord, which he expanded later by purchasing an additional thirteen acres. Still a happy family, the Hawthornes enjoyed walks to Walden Pond, Sleepy Hollow, and their former home, Old Manse. Among their neighbors were horticulturist Ephraim Bull, who developed the Concord grape, and the Emersons. The only blot on their happiness at Wayside was the death of Hawthorne's sister Maria Louisa in a boat accident on the Hudson River.

When Hawthorne moved back to Concord, he wrote *The Blithedale Romance*, a thinly disguised story about his experiences at Brook Farm ten years earlier. It was published in America on July 14, 1852, and later in London. This book was less well received than were *The Scarlet Letter* and *The House of the Seven Gables*. By June 1852, Hawthorne's college friend Franklin Pierce had won the Democratic nomination for president. Having offered his help, Hawthorne wrote a campaign biography of Pierce, which he completed at the end of August 1852. Hawthorne wanted Pierce to win the election and offer him an appointment in England so that he could visit the homeland of his ancestors and travel to scenes described in English literature. After Pierce had won the election and granted Hawthorne's wish, Hawthorne wrote *Tanglewood Tales* while waiting to leave for a consulship in Liverpool, England. Similar to *A Wonder-Book*, this collection of tales also adapted Greek myths for children. It was published in August 1853 both in America and in England.

THE HAWTHORNES IN EUROPE

After renting Wayside to Sophia's brother Nathaniel, the Hawthornes sailed from Boston for Liverpool on July 6, 1853, on the steamer *Niagra*, a voyage that took ten days. Hawthorne began work on August 1 in an office near the Liverpool docks. His job as consul consisted of keeping accounts, processing documents, and listening to the complaints of American sailors who had been mistreated on ships that docked in Liverpool. The job was hard and unpleasant, but Hawthorne performed his duties well in the tradition taught him years earlier by his uncle Robert Manning. His consulship ended in 1857. While in England, the Hawthornes visited Shakespeare country, the Lake District of William Wordsworth, London, the Scottish Highlands, and many other sites. Hawthorne's only writing while in England was *The English Notebook*. From England, the family traveled to Paris for sightseeing before going on to Rome.

The Hawthornes spent a year in Rome, a plan that was Sophia's dream. It was a time for sightseeing and journal writing. The Rome trip was thoroughly documented in Nathaniel's and Sophia's journals and in the letters of the children's tutor, Ada Shepard, to her fiancé, Clay Badger. Hawthorne visited American artists, who had found Rome a congenial place to gather and study. One of them, Maria Louise Lander of Salem, became the model for Hilda, a character in *The Marble Faun*, which Hawthorne set in Rome. Because of his interest in religion, Hawthorne studied Catholicism while in Rome. In particular, he studied the Catholic practice of confession and its effect in alleviating guilt. Except for an eight-day sightseeing trip to Florence, the Hawthornes stayed in Rome until May 1859.

The Hawthornes planned a brief stop in England before they returned to America, but when they got to London, the London publishers Smith and Elder offered Hawthorne £600 for a new romance, an offer Hawthorne accepted. Since he had started a draft of *The Marble Faun* in Italy, he went to York in the north of England on July 26 to finish it. The book was published on February 28, 1860, under the title *Transformations*. It came out in Boston a few days later as *The Marble Faun*. The Hawthornes finally sailed for America from Liverpool on June 16, 1860, on the steamship *Europa*.

THE LAST YEARS

The Hawthornes arrived at Wayside in Concord to a warm welcome home after an absence of seven years. The ensuing months were taken up with an active social life with their transcendentalist friends and Boston publishers. Gradually Hawthorne returned to writing, using his English notebooks as a basis for magazine pieces. In 1863, he published *Our Old Home*, a collection of sketches describing his observations and experiences in England. He made four attempts to write another novel, but he was unable to work out his complicated plot and theme to his satisfaction. These manuscripts were eventually published posthumously. As the year progressed, Hawthorne became weak, sick, and depressed and could no longer write, but he refused to see a doctor. In May 1864, even though he was not feeling well, Hawthorne went on a trip with Franklin Pierce, whose wife had died a year earlier. They met in Boston and boarded a train, planning stops on the way to Concord, New Hampshire, Pierce's home. On May 18, they stopped in Plymouth, New Hampshire. Between three and four in the morning of May 19, Pierce went to Hawthorne's room to check on him and found Hawthorne dead. He would have been sixty years old on July 4, 1864. He was buried on May 23 in Concord, Massachusetts.

After Hawthorne's death, Sophia edited and published her husband's notebooks. Then, in 1868, she left Concord to live in Dresden, Germany. In 1870, she moved to London, where she died a year later. Una, who was with her mother, worked in London, never married, and died in 1877. Julian wrote a two-volume biography of his parents, entitled *Nathaniel Hawthorne and His Wife*. He lived until 1933. Rose, after an unhappy marriage, worked in a Catholic home for cancer patients until her death in 1938.

ABOUT THIS BOOK

The biography of Nathaniel Hawthorne is designed to provide students with the basic facts about Hawthorne's life: when and where he lived and a record of his writing career. In addition, it provides numerous experiences and anecdotes to enlighten the personality of Hawthorne as a writer and interpretations of his works. More attention has been given to the years from his birth through 1851, when he published *The House of the Seven Gables*. These years cover his early development as a writer and the publication of the tales and novels most frequently studied by high school students. His later years and works are also important, but they are more often the subject matter of advanced Hawthorne studies.

The essays and reviews selected for the Literary Companion to Nathaniel Hawthorne provide teachers and students with a wide range of information and opinion about Hawthorne and his works. Some of the selections offer insight into the way Hawthorne's personal life contributed to his works. Some analyze the philosophical outlook Hawthorne presents through his fiction. A few essayists and reviewers rate the quality of Hawthorne's art and rank him as a literary artist. Several essays analyze the characters, themes, and literary techniques of particular works. Students will find in this collection abundant material to pique their interest and stimulate ideas for research papers or oral presentations.

This collection is loosely organized in three sections. Essays about Hawthorne's sources of material, his philosophical outlook, and his ranking as an artist appear in the first third of the book. Discussions of literary techniques within various stories and novels appear in the middle. And analyses of *The Scarlet Letter* appear last. Because *The Scarlet Letter* is Hawthorne's most highly rated work, four essays focus on various elements of it.

Most of the authors of the essays and reviews collected for this volume are twentieth-century writers. Renewed interest in Nathaniel Hawthorne accompanied the centenary of the publication of *The Scarlet Letter* in 1950 and the centenary of the author's death in 1964; during those decades scholars published many new studies. Two essays in this collection, however, were written by Hawthorne's contemporaries. Edgar Allan Poe is famous for refining the structure of the short story; in 1842, he reviewed Hawthorne's tales in light of that structure. And Hawthorne's friend Herman Melville, author of *Moby-Dick*, and, like Hawthorne, fascinated by themes of guilt and redemption, reviewed other tales. Both Poe and Melville saw greater art and a greater depth of spirit in Hawthorne than most critics had yet seen. Moreover, both Poe and Melville judged Hawthorne an outstanding writer before the publication of *The Scarlet Letter.*

The Literary Companion to Nathaniel Hawthorne has several special features. The introduction to each essay summarizes the main points so that the reader knows what to expect. Interspersed within the essays, the reader will find inserts that support the essay, add supplementary information, or provide interesting anecdotes. Inserts come from sources such as historical and religious writings of early Puritan leaders, Hawthorne's notebooks, and newspaper reviews from the time *The Scarlet Letter* was published.

Stories Derived from New England Living

Edmund Fuller and B. Jo Kinnick

In the introduction to their collection of Nathaniel Hawthorne's short stories, Edmund Fuller and B. Jo Kinnick describe Hawthorne as a quiet and thoughtful man who found subject matter for stories close to home. He roamed New England's farms, docks, markets, and taverns observing local citizens and listening to their tales. Using his imagination to enhance these experiences, he wrote stories of fantasy and morality, many of which, such as "Ethan Brand" and "Dr. Heidegger's Experiment," make creative use of symbols. Hawthorne shared qualities of writing with Edgar Allan Poe and influenced Herman Melville, both of whom were important writers of the romantic period.

Visitors to Salem, Massachusetts, can see a fascinating old gray house with all the characteristics, inside and out, of early Puritan architecture. Its interest is heightened by certain mysterious panels and hidden passages. It is called "The House of the Seven Gables," and it is the traditional site of Hawthorne's famous, mystery-haunted novel of that name.

The House of the Seven Gables deals with the effects of a curse, and though the tale itself is fiction, the germ of the story sprang from the author's family history. One of Nathaniel Hawthorne's ancestors was Judge Hathorne, who presided at the notorious Salem witch trials and was put under a curse by the husband of one of the convicted witches. (The ghost of Judge Hathorne presides over the trial in "The Devil and Daniel Webster," [a story by modern writer Stephen Vincent Benét].) The spelling of the family name remained Hathorne until young Nathaniel inserted the "w."

Nathaniel Hawthorne was born in Salem in 1804. In his

Excerpted from *Adventures in American Literature*, Laureate Edition, by Edmund Fuller and B. Jo Kinnick, Mary Rives Bowman, and Herbert Potell; copyright ©1963 by Harcourt Brace & Company and renewed 1991 by Jesica Sand, Lydia Winderman, Edmund Fuller, Mary Rives Bowman, Florence E. Potell. Reprinted by permission of the publisher.

youth the town was a port whose glory had departed. There had been an era when the ship lanes had linked Salem with every remote and romantic place on earth; when spices, silks, ivories, teas, and other precious stuffs were piled on its wharves; when the face of almost every race of man could be seen in its narrow streets. Now in the shifts of wealth and commerce, Boston and other ports had surpassed Salem. Its trade dwindled to a trickle and finally stopped altogether. Hawthorne, in "The Custom House," the introductory chapter to *The Scarlet Letter*, described the old employees of the shipping office rocking in rows of chairs, mostly idle now in a town where once there had been a scurrying hustle.

Hawthorne's father, a sea captain, had died of yellow fever in Dutch Guiana, when the boy was a mere four years old. When the news came of his father's death, Hawthorne's mother withdrew into her upstairs bedroom, coming out only rarely during the remaining forty years of her life. The boy and his two sisters lived in almost complete isolation from her and from each other. In a few years Hawthorne left Salem and entered Bowdoin College, in Maine. . . .

GATHERING MATERIAL FOR STORIES

From Bowdoin Hawthorne returned to Salem. For nearly twelve years, from 1825 to 1836, he lived in virtual solitude in this idle town. Unlike his friend [and fellow author] Herman Melville, who traveled widely and observed much in his youth, there was little in his own actual experiences as yet to serve as literary material. Hawthorne gathered his material by observing and listening to others. He roamed around the town, moving among old sailors on the docks, farmers from the country, men clustered in taverns, and the old wives of the town at the market. He listened to all of them. Their talk was filled with New England lore, legend, and superstition. He made annual excursions into Vermont and New Hampshire and absorbed hints for many stories on these jaunts. He also read the annals and chronicles of the Puritan world. He filled his notebooks and his thoughts with these scraps of impressions and memories, and after a few years began pouring them out as marvelously wrought tales.

During this period in Salem, Hawthorne had harvested the richness of his background. Then a sound instinct made him leave the town where his ancestors had dwelt for two centuries. In "The Custom House," he remarks, "Human nature will not flourish any more than a potato, if it be planted and replanted, for too long a series of generations, in the same worn-out soil." In this chapter, too, he reveals the depth of his concern with the dark side of Puritanism, the harshness and the persecutions. He says of his ancestors, especially Judge Hathorne, "I . . . hereby take shame upon myself for their sakes, and pray that any curse incurred by them . . . may be now and henceforth removed.". . .

TRAVELING AND OBSERVING

Nathaniel Hawthorne, whose uncle Samuel Manning owned stagecoach lines, enjoyed traveling on his uncle's stages to see the countryside and observe New England village life. His note-book observations of these trips served as material for his stories. On July 27, 1838, he recorded this description of Pittsfield, a village in western Massachusetts.

The central square of Pittsfield presents all the bustle of a thriving village—the farmers of the vicinity in light wagons, sulkies, or on horseback; stages at the door of the Berkshire Hotel, under the stoop of which sit or lounge the guests, stage-people, and idlers, observing or assisting the arrivals and departures—huge trunks and bandboxes unladed [unloaded] and laded. The courtesy shown to ladies in assisting them to alight, in a shower, under umbrellas. The dull looks of passengers, who have ridden all night, scarcely brightened by the excitement of arriving at a new place. The stage agent demanding the names of those who are going on:—some to Lebanon Springs, some to Albany. The toddy-stick [bartender] is still busy at these Berkshire public houses. At dinner, soup preliminary, in city style—guests, the court-people, [editor Charles Frederick] Briggs, member of congress, attending a trial here; horse-dealers, country squires, store-keepers in the village &c &c. My room, a narrow crib, overlooking a back court-yard, where a young man and a lad were drawing water for the maid-servants.

Nathaniel Hawthorne, *The American Notebooks.* Edited by Randall Stewart. New Haven, CT: Yale University Press, 1932.

He lived for a few months in 1841 at Brook Farm, one of the famous New England experiments in communal living, where some of the region's most remarkable, if somewhat impractical, people gathered. Hawthorne was essentially of a solitary nature, and group life was not for him, but the experience provided the material for his later novel *The Blithedale Romance* (1852). In 1841 he married Sophia Peabody, of a prominent Salem family. For some three years Hawthorne and Sophia lived in the house called the Old Manse, in Concord. It was there that he wrote the splendid stories in the volume called *Mosses from an Old Manse* (1846). . . .

HAWTHORNE'S SYMBOLIC STORIES

Hawthorne's unique gift was for the creation of strongly symbolic stories which touch the deepest roots of man's moral nature. The finest example is the re-creation of Puritan Boston, *The Scarlet Letter*. In this novel each word, image, and event works toward a single effect. It is a complex story of guilt, its effects upon various persons, and how deliverance is obtained for some of them.

His ability to create vivid and symbolic images that embody great moral questions appears strongly in his short stories. In "Ethan Brand" a marble heart stands for pride and isolation from one's fellow men. "Young Goodman Brown" uses the background of witchcraft to explore uncertainties of belief that trouble a man's heart and mind. "Dr. Heidegger's Experiment" and "The Ambitious Guest" have symbolic and legendary qualities. "The Great Stone Face" is another of his allegorical stories.

It was Hawthorne's ability to make a story exist in its own right but at the same time appear as a moral symbol that most influenced the work of Herman Melville. Melville called his friend "the largest brain with the largest heart" in American literature. Hawthorne shares with Edgar Allan Poe the distinction of advancing the art of the short story, giving to the form qualities that are uniquely American. Like Poe he often used grotesque or fantastic events, but Hawthorne's work is broader in range and has more depth of thought. Poe was concerned with the immediate emotional effects of literature and often seemed indifferent to investigations of value or morality. To Hawthorne and Melville, however, the telling of a tale was a way of inquiring into the meaning of life.

The Divided Artist and His Uncles

Gloria C. Erlich

Nathaniel Hawthorne expressed uncertainty about his worth as a writer even after his early tales had succeeded with readers. Some critics dismiss his professions of self-doubt as insincere posturing. Gloria C. Erlich, in *Family Themes and Hawthorne's Fiction: The Tenacious Web*, argues instead that Hawthorne's uncertainty was genuine and that it resulted from the opposing influences of two of his uncles. One uncle, Samuel Manning, fostered Hawthorne's rootless, artistic tendency. On the other hand, his uncle Robert Manning, who was stern and puritanical, instilled in Hawthorne doubt about the legitimacy of fiction writing as a profession. Erlich examines the play of these two conflicting forces in Hawthorne's tales for "The Story Teller" sequence.

Despite the genuine achievements of his early tales, between the ages of forty-one and forty-five, Hawthorne was weighing his literary accomplishment and finding it insubstantial. Critics like to dismiss his self-deprecations as a pose, an artfully constructed persona of the prefaces with little or no biographical significance. But even a persona is related to the self; it is a selection from and a heightening of genuine personality traits. Even when Hawthorne whimsically exaggerates his trifling, he refers to genuine concerns about himself. Moreover, the author as idle trifler [of slight worth] is not a notion peculiar to the prefaces; it was a figure of long-standing concern in Hawthorne's fiction as well. The literary expressions of Hawthorne's misgivings about his manliness, his seriousness, and the value of his profession are rooted in life experience.

He depicts the fiction creator as socially marginal at least as

Excerpted from Gloria C. Erlich, *Family Themes and Hawthorne's Fiction: The Tenacious Web*; ©1984 by Rutgers—The State University. Reprinted by permission of Rutgers University Press.

early as "The Story Teller" sequence, a product of his late twenties. This fragmentary collection of framed tales [individual stories united by a single element or frame] was one of his attempts to fuse a solid literary work out of separate stories after the fashion of [American writer] Washington Irving. Failure to get the frame and stories published together was a great setback to his ambition to produce a substantial work. The extant parts of the frame narrative reveal a storyteller who feels vocationally diminished by contrast to the more manly and imposing figure of his guardian, Parson Thumpcushion, as well as by other substantial men of affairs.

In "Passages from a Relinquished Work," probably intended as the opening of the frame narrative, we can see the author's sincere attempt to do justice to a very troubling presence in the life of an orphaned young artist. The narrator conveys, in addition to the Parson's emphatic personality and oppressive presence, a balancing sense of his decency, good intentions, and generosity, trying to attribute to the difficulties of a guardian-ward relationship the conflicts that each experienced with the other. Although the Parson's firm convictions about the proper vocation for a young man did not prevail over the young artist's intentions, they effectively undermined his valuation of his own talents. The Parson insisted on the young man's "adopting a particular profession," whereas the future Story Teller was determined to "keep aloof from the regular business of life."

Although the Story Teller leaves home for life on the road, he is unable to escape the Parson's image of the artist as an idler, a word associated with fiction-mongering even up to the time of "The Custom-House." He felt ranked with libertines [one who acts without restraint] and paupers, "with the drunken poet, who hawked his own fourth of July odes." The negative image inculcated by his guardian pursues the young man who fled home in order to escape it. The narrator's first friend on the road, his fellow traveler and later competitor for audience attention, is a young divine [theologian or minister] who combines the Story Teller's alter ego with a youthful incarnation of the Parson. In high spirits and full of confidence that his "idle trade" demands the highest mental and emotional capacities, the Story Teller learns that his first performance is to be with a British company entertaining at a tavern. In this liberated atmosphere, his fellow performers turn out to be "of doubtful sex," and the Story Teller enjoys the unnerving success of being appreciated for the wrong reasons.

After the performance, the Story Teller receives a letter from Parson Thumpcushion that he burns without reading, but by which he is profoundly affected. "I seemed to see the Puritanic figure of my guardian, standing among the fripperies [shallow, showy people] of the theatre, and pointing to the players,—the fantastic and effeminate men, the painted women, the giddy girl in boy's clothes, merrier than modest,—pointing to these with solemn ridicule, and eyeing me with stern rebuke. His image was a type of the austere duty, and they of the vanities of life." Needless to say, the licentious image spoiled the Story Teller's taste for his chosen profession.

"Passages" attempts levity but clearly wrestles with a young writer's genuine feelings about his stern but benevolent father-surrogate. In implying that such a guardian can become a *Doppelgänger* [alter ego], an internalized figure whose memory converts artistic endeavor into vanity if not depravity, Hawthorne was coming dangerously close to private experience. Little wonder that he relinquished the work.

In *The Shape of Hawthorne's Career*, critic Nina Baym asserts repeatedly that much of Hawthorne's writing before *The Scarlet Letter* tamely follows what he conceived to be audience expectations and therefore deprecates imagination and extolls the common destiny of ordinary mankind. In contrast to those who attribute biographical significance to "Passages," she denies that it could represent more than a minor aspect of Hawthorne's personality. But in discussing the *Twice-Told Tales* period, she declares, "Hawthorne's sketches represent a voluntary repression of a powerful talent that is astonishing in its perversity. No audience would have demanded from him the concessions that he made in advance. . . . We cannot wonder that he always wrote with an audience in mind; but we have to wonder at the severity of his conception of that audience." She attributes to Hawthorne's inexperience of the world his imperfect understanding of his audience, and then explains his repression of the imagination by saying that in ignorance of his real audience, he invented a readership "composed of rational teachers and stern ministers—a readership of Parson Thumpcushions!"

THE INFLUENCE OF THE MANNING UNCLES

Such repression of the imagination as we find in Hawthorne is more likely due to involuntary forces than to concessions to audience expectations. Indeed, his repressive Puritans who make the fiction writer feel trivial are probably transformed images of his own guardian, Robert Manning, rather than of an inaccurately perceived audience of readers. Robert Manning was not in fact unimaginative or even opposed to imagination, but with his artistic nephew he took a stern and puritanical line.

THE CRITICAL MANNINGS

After Nathaniel Hawthorne's mother moved to Maine in 1816, Nathaniel and his two sisters stayed much of the time with the Robert Manning family in Salem, Massachusetts. All of the children missed their mother and complained of the Mannings' harshness and criticism. Hawthorne's letter of March 7, 1820, when he was fifteen years old, reveals his displeasure.

March 7th 1820

Mr. Oliver thought I could enter College next commencement, but Uncle Robert is afraid I should have to study too hard. I get my lessons at home, and recite them to him at 7 o'clock in the morning. I am extremely homesick. Aunt Mary is continually scolding at me. Grandmaam hardly ever speaks a pleasant word to me. If I ever attempt to speak a word in my defense, they cry out against my impudence. However I guess I can live through a year and a half more, and then I shall leave them. One good effect results from their eternal finding-fault. It gives me some employment in retaliating, and that keeps up my spirits. Mother I wish you would let Louisa board with Mrs. Dike if she comes up here to go to school. Then Aunt M. can't have her to domineer over. I hope, however, that I shall see none of you up here very soon.

Gloria C. Erlich, *Family Themes and Hawthorne's Fiction: The Tenacious Web.* New Brunswick, NJ: Rutgers University Press, 1984.

The Mannings were known for their "sensibility" as well as for their business acumen, and Robert Manning exemplified both. He was an extremely capable and prudent businessman, but he also devoted both money and energy to the cultivation of fruit trees. A person who readily and naturally assumed responsibility, he directed the Manning family business after the death of his father, and, although not the oldest son, he became the man in the lives of his sister's young family after [Nathaniel Hawthorne's father] Captain Hathorne's death. Robert Manning made the essential decisions in the lives of the Hawthorne children and is well known as the uncle who sent Hawthorne to college. We shall see that he also assumed responsibility for Hawthorne's early education and often came between the boy and his mother. Robert Manning tended to be playful and loving with his Hawthorne nieces but was quite strict with young Nathaniel.

Although Hawthorne respected the motives of his Uncle Robert, he often longed to be free of his tyranny and his values. For such a dreamy boy, an uncle who was always keeping him to the grindstone must have seemed very puritanical indeed. Young Hawthorne felt more kinship with the renegade Uncle Samuel, much closer to his own age, who liked taverns, story swapping, the irregular life of the road. In fact, the Manning family plotted regularly to bring Samuel into line. They tried in vain to keep him employed in Uncle Richard's general store in Maine in the hope that he would settle down.

Often accompanying Samuel on his horse-buying trips, young Nathaniel formed a strong bond with him against the strict Manning code of hard work, sobriety, and religion. The dream of being a vagabond storyteller derives from this happy association, which terminated with Samuel's early death. Samuel was never tamed by Manning values and did not live to pay the price of living outside them. Internalized as a joyful figure of vagabond irresponsibility, this uncle remained part of his nephew's psyche as an impulse toward rootlessness. Continually changing residences, Hawthorne called the only home he ever owned "The Wayside" and was eventually to die in a wayside hotel. "The Story Teller" dramatizes the influence of both uncles in the form of joyous digressions from the bourgeois [middle class] ideal shadowed by figures representing the puritan conscience.

THE DIVIDED ARTIST

Also a part of "The Story Teller" sequence, "The Seven Vagabonds" depicts another version of the same polarity. The narrator is a young man "in the spring of [his] life and the summer of the year" at a crossroad of three directions. He is drawn toward a caravan, a house on wheels, operated by a traveling showman and an itinerant bookseller, and shortly thereafter joined by a con man, a fiddler, operators of a show-box, all of them aspects of the artist. Attracted by their gay, spontaneous way of life, and by the notion of a home on wheels, he wishes to join this carefree band. The old showman questions his fitness for the role of roving entertainer; he finds the narrator merely a "strolling gentleman" in contrast with respectable vagabonds who get their "bread in some creditable way. Every honest man should have his livelihood." On the spot, the wanderer invents the vocation of traveling storyteller in order to establish respectability with this motley crew. Only with the aid of an advocate among them is he accepted by the band headed for a camp meeting. Joyful at having joined a society of outsiders, the narrator feels at one with their world until he spies a horseman approaching from the direction of the camp meeting. A Methodist minister sitting his horse with "rigid perpendicularity, a tall thin figure in rusty black," this priestly spoilsport brings word that the camp meeting has broken up. The merry group disbands, blasted by the Methodist's grim visage.

Even among vagabonds, the Story Teller feels trivial and suspect. He lacks a "creditable" livelihood and seems not entirely one of them. This youth choosing a direction in the spring of his life reminds one of another divided artist figure, Thomas Mann's Tonio Kröger, whose honesty is suspected even on a visit to his home town, and who is always associated with a gypsy in a green wagon. Neither others nor he himself can quite believe in his respectability. This divided artist is rejected by both communities, the bourgeois and the bohemian [nonconformist with literary and artistic interests].

Thomas Mann attributed his own and his protagonists' guilty identities as artists to the split inherited from [comfortable, middle-class] burgher fathers and bohemian mothers. In Hawthorne a similar mentality obtained, but in the case of this fatherless boy, it is more likely derived from the influence of two important uncles—the carefree Samuel and the eminently respectable Robert. If Uncle Samuel fostered the rootless vagabond tendency, Uncle Robert, with the values of the whole Manning clan behind him, could well have been transformed into the censoring puritanical figures who, under various guises, often ministerial, make the impecunious artist feel like an idler, a mere "fiddler," a lightweight, and a man of uncertain masculinity.

In a sense Hawthorne was transmuting his two uncles into psychic symbols of an archetypal polarity—the Dionysian [pleasure-seeking abandon] and the Apollonian [ordered, balanced harmony], primitivism and civilization, self and society. These opposing forces meet in full panoply in "The Maypole of Merrymount," another early work. In the contest for empire between jollity and gloom, "jollity" manages in the course of description to incorporate the decorative arts (as opposed to the functional), carnival, masquerade, fantasy, and, above all, sexual license with the unmistakable implication of sexual ambiguity. Indulgence runs amok, allowing the author license to revel in the pleasures of unrestraint before closing in with the forces of repression. When, after pages of inventive revelry, Governor Endicott finally enters the circle, "no fantastic foolery could look him in the face. So stern was the energy of his aspect, that the whole man, visage, frame, and soul, seemed wrought of iron, gifted with life and thought, yet all of one substance with his head-piece and breast-plate. It was the Puritan of Puritans."

THE TRIUMPH OF DISCIPLINE

The triumph of discipline was inevitable; few can imagine adult human life as endless play. Revelry must end, children must grow up, Edens must be forfeited for a world of sober work. And, because the polarities do represent two genuine aspects of human nature, neither of which can be totally denied, even Endicott of the armored head and heart and soul of iron softened his strictures to bring them within tolerable human limits. Even the "severest Puritan of all" knew enough to garland the heads of the newlyweds with "roses from the ruin of the Maypole." Perhaps only the truly disciplined, like Governor Endicott, Hawthorne, and Thomas Mann, know how to value the sensuality that is restrained by iron bands of control.

Toadying to an unimaginative audience was not the reason Hawthorne's earlier tales conclude with control of the forces of extravagance, ambition, or imagination and advocate settling for the normal course of human existence within social boundaries. On the contrary, he let his more extravagant characters test the unlimited for him and sadly concluded that it was unlivable.

Moreover, like most of us, Hawthorne had within him an image of restraint and responsibility that made it impossible for him to give free rein to the Byronic impulses [free, unrestrained, from British poet Lord Byron] that he personified in Oberon, hero of "The Devil in Manuscript." Not only was Hawthorne a descendant of founders of New England society, he was also reared in the very middle-class home of the Mannings. He could safely play with the fantasy of vagabondage just as he could safely play with the fantasy of Oberon, the doomed poet, whose early death and touching literary remains would wrench the hearts of his unappreciative family. He could entertain these identities imaginatively, *because* he was safely anchored in the bourgeois tradition, had "some slender means" inherited from these bourgeois earnings, and had received enough discipline from his unappreciated Uncle Robert that he could earn his own living when necessary.

Hawthorne's harsh portrait of Endicott in "The Maypole of Merrymount" is tempered by recognition that such iron men form the basis of social structures. Such disciplinarians seem most like iron men, most repressive, to those driven by urgent impulses. Note, therefore, the description of Governor Endicott—his sternness, his energy, his iron soul, and the unity of his armored personality. So forceful that fantastic foolery could not confront it, this personality is the prototype of the iron men who appear in various guises throughout Hawthorne's work. Whether merchants, blacksmiths, monomaniac philanthropists, ministers, or Puritan fathers, they invariably make artisans of the imagination feel trivial, unworthy, and unmanly.

Hawthorne's Puritan Mind

Stanley T. Williams

Stanley T. Williams's essay on Nathaniel Hawthorne's
Puritan mind is excerpted from a much longer essay in
which Williams analyzes how solitude contributed to
Hawthorne's work. Forced by family circumstances to
spend his childhood alone, Hawthorne learned how to
teach himself. Later, for more than a decade, he held a
solitary customhouse job in Salem, Massachusetts.
There he reflected on his Puritan ancestors and practiced his writing skills. He emerged from this quiet
period with several tales and a novel, *The Scarlet Letter*,
that reveal the mind of New England Puritanism. The
naturalness of his art—his deeply human characters
and his fidelity to no style of expression but his own—
distinguishes Hawthorne as an important nineteenth-
century writer, according to Williams.

Soon after Hawthorne's birth in 1804, circumstances intensi-
fied his innate Puritan characteristics: his analysis of the
mind, his somber outlook on living, his tendency to withdraw
from his fellows. Yet if, from the first, in the quiet household
of his widowed mother at Salem, during a period of lameness
which kept him out of sports, or throughout the summers in
remote Raymond, Maine, he became increasingly introspective, he had few personal problems of mind or spirit. Already
he was detached. . . . These "accursed habits" of solitude, as
he once called them, failed to make him unhappy. In them, as
a matter of fact, lay the origins of his life of the intellect and
spirit. Out of such habits, formed in the first twenty-one years
of his life, were to be born Ethan Brand, Hester Prynne,
Zenobia, and the other lonely children of his imagination. . . .

There remained only one step to fix him in this course of
life; and this he took on his return from Brunswick [Maine,

where Hawthorne attended college]: he became a "Salemite." For, he said, "I felt it almost as a destiny to make Salem my home." The quiet streets, the lonely house, the necessity for solitude, and his innate passion for the written word, all counseled a procedure whose continuance for twelve long years has never been satisfactorily explained. Probably the reasons are not really mysterious: presumably, he had experienced no romantic disillusionment nor grief. Those eyes which Bayard Taylor [writer of travel books] said could flash fire, never viewed coldly men's lives in the busy world. Perhaps, as he wrote [Henry Wadsworth] Longfellow later, he merely drifted into this role of recluse. Or perhaps—why not, if we think of

SATAN AND WITCHCRAFT

To the New England Puritans, Satan was real and his work-ings in their community caused witchcraft. In an excerpt from The Wonders of the Invisible World, *written in 1692, just after the Salem witchcraft trials ended, Cotton Mather warns colonists about Satan's second attempt to cause trouble among them. One of Nathaniel Hawthorne's ancestors was a judge who prosecuted the alleged witches.*

Wherefore the devil is now making one attempt more upon us, an attempt more difficult, more surprising, more snarled with unintelligible circumstances than any that we have hith-erto encountered, an attempt so critical, that if we get well through, we shall soon enjoy halcyon days with all the vul-tures of hell trodden under our feet. He has wanted his incar-nate legions to persecute us, as the people of God have in the other hemisphere been persecuted. He has therefore drawn forth his more spiritual ones to make an attack upon us. We have been advised by some credible Christians yet alive, that a malefactor, accused of witchcraft as well as murder, and exe-cuted in this place more than forty years ago, did then give notice of an horrible plot against the country by witchcraft, and a foundation of witchcraft then laid, which if it were not seasonably discovered, would probably blow up and pull down all the churches in the country. And we have now with horror seen the discovery of such a witchcraft! An army of devils is horribly broke in upon the place which is the center and, after a sort, the firstborn of our English settlements, and the houses of the good people there are filled with the doleful shrieks of their children and servants, tormented by invisible hands, with tortures altogether preternatural.

Cotton Mather, *The Wonders of the Invisible World,* in *Anthology of American Literature,* edited by George McMichael. 2nd ed. Vol. 1. New York: Macmillan, 1980.

his satisfaction in his later fame?—he meant in this Philistine America to glean the rewards of his painful solitude; namely, independence and literary success. At any rate, here he sat long in his "accustomed chamber," writing, revising, and burning the sketches and tales; perfecting his delicate craft of the symbol, of allegory, of the few themes and oft repeated character-types which were to haunt forever the minds of those who know New England.

When in 1837 he emerged from the chamber where his "fame was won," in his hand was his first published collection of prose, *Twice-Told Tales*, and primarily in his heart the image of Sophia Peabody, to whom he was married five years later, with enriching consequences to his personal life and to his writing. Neither his recognition as an author (by [Edgar Allan] Poe, among others) nor his new, happy companionship in a solitude which he never really relinquished, altered his literary aims. He was, like his own Holgrave in *The House of the Seven Gables*, deepened and softened; but his broadening through associations with the workaday world as a measurer in the Boston Customhouse, as a laborer in the Brook Farm Community, and as a surveyor in the Salem Customhouse seems, in retrospect, illusory. . . .

In 1849 he sat down and, using the craft he had learned in silence, wrote, hardly blotting a line; in four months he had finished *The Scarlet Letter*. The mid-century mark and the two following years beheld the apogee of Hawthorne's art (*The Scarlet Letter*, *The House of the Seven Gables*, and *The Blithedale Romance*, as well as his best collection of tales); and the decade was rounded out by his exquisite, if rather tired, study of Puritanism in a Latin environment, *The Marble Faun* (1860). The lacuna [gap] of eight years in his formal writing we owe to a sudden dislocation in his New England life: his appointment by President Franklin Pierce to the American consulship in Liverpool, with a subsequent sojourn in Italy. . . .

THE INFLUENCE OF HAWTHORNE'S PURITAN PAST

In any study of Hawthorne's art, his life story must be regarded as causative. Fixed from birth in his Puritan attitudes, he would, we may believe, have been Hawthorne had he lived for many years upon the *rive gauche* [left bank of the Seine River in Paris] or the banks of the Mississippi. It was so in Rome; Italy failed to alter the underlying mechanisms of his Puritan mind. For he was completely integrated, until his fiftieth year, with the soil and spirit of a New England which had bred and indoctrinated his introspective forebears. He was not unlike Major William Hathorne, that "grave, bearded, sabled-cloaked and steeple-crowned progenitor,—who came so early [to America], with his Bible and his sword," or his ancestor Judge Hathorne, the persecutor of witches. Such antecedents continued to be a powerful influence in his character as a writer. We can understand New England without Hawthorne; yet Hawthorne without New England we cannot comprehend. She was literally of his blood and brain; her scenes and her people form the stuff of his romances, and his own forefathers revisit the upper shades in his pages. What he wrote of New England was not merely "local color"; rather it was the subconscious mind of New England. . . .

It was this memorable art of his which distinguished him from [Ralph Waldo] Emerson and [Henry David] Thoreau, an art which included his distillations of historical episodes into moods; soft color schemes of red, white, and black; rhythms of sentence and phrase which echo the harmony of his unified and reposeful life; symbols, sometimes inadequate and even absurd, but more often coefficients of the unseen moral laws which he was trying to communicate; and unforgettable case histories of men and women afflicted by guilt, or, as he called it, by "a stain upon the soul." Little of this he drew from books, apart from his beloved [John] Bunyan, from [John] Milton, or from [Edmund] Spenser [sixteenth- and seventeenth-century English writers], who inspired some of his allegory and even the name of one of his daughters, Una. From common incidents and from common men he wove his intricate web of the seemingly inevitable involutions of the moral pattern. Yes, except for an excusable contamination of the didactic [inclined to teach or moralize] in a few tales which he composed during his period of apprenticeship, he maintained toward all his laboratory researches into the human heart a singular detachment. His were grave and acute reflections upon the way in which the Puritan mind worked; it was, for almost the first time in American literary history, as the devoted Henry James was quick to see, the judgment of the artist upon familiar Puritan material. Thus he was akin to Poe; he anticipated James himself; and he was really the founder of the psychological novel in America. . . .

TALES AND NOVEL PORTRAY PURITAN MIND

The tales [short stories] emphasize Hawthorne's matchless delineation of Puritanism in the seventeenth century. They constitute a minor compensation for the fact that only one of his novels deals with this epoch, with which, by reason of reading and temperament, he was so deeply familiar. "The Maypole of Merrymount," "The Gray Champion," "Howe's Masquerade," all historical pieces, give us the fruits of his profound knowledge of his ancestors' world, and intensify our regret that only *The Scarlet Letter* (though this is much) exists, among his major writings, to demonstrate his extraordinary gift for re-creating the world of the Winthrops and the Mathers [Puritan leaders in Massachusetts colony]. These seventeenth-century tales are relatively few, but they have come to be a precious frame of reference for the great novel. Because of them we view it with more understanding, and had they never been written it assuredly would be less. Hawthorne pondered much on these Puritan precursors of his; he even wondered whimsically what they would have thought of him, their renegade romancer-descendant. Why in 1850 after the publication of *The Scarlet Letter* he wrote no more novels concerning seventeenth-century Puritanism remains an enigma. The deeper Hawthorne resided in this period, and the tales concerning it are essential to our understanding of him. . . .

In 1849 Hawthorne wrote in effortless fashion, after his long indenture to such themes and characters, *The Scarlet Letter*, his lovely novel "of human frailty and sorrow." It is too easy, from the moment that we mingle at the prison door with the women in hoods and the men in gray steeple-crowned hats until we stand beside Hester Prynne's grave, to undervalue Hawthorne's superb interfusion of fact and fancy in this tale of New England seventeenth-century life: sincere in its way and aspiring, but brutish too, and often debasing, save as it could provoke the "spiritual warfare" in Hester's breast. What Hawthorne conveys of the olden time is less literal—though this element is also present, for example, in the portraits of Governor Bellingham or Mistress Hibbins—than might have been predicted from his skillful distillation of history in "The Maypole of Merrymount." Such modes of thought, our reading and the Puritan inheritance in our own minds confirm as true. There is no heavy-handed intrusion of theological doctrine or of local custom. Church, priest, sermon, court of justice, and meetinghouse are here, but all are incidental to a persuasive reality of mind. Pearl could have passed an examination in *The New England Primer* or the Westminster Catechism; but Pearl is a living child, not an animated monograph on the nature of Puritan children. All that Hawthorne had heard by word of mouth of this past, all that he had read in the Mathers or [New England historian] Thomas Prince, and all that he had divined through his own mind of the Puritans, make the background of *The Scarlet Letter* as accurate as a town record but also as alive as the grim beadle [church usher] himself or comely Hester Prynne. Perhaps the primary virtue of *The Scarlet Letter* is stylistic: its unity and perfection of tone. . . .

Any survey of *The Scarlet Letter* returns us ultimately to the ever-present inner compulsion in Hawthorne toward that frontier of human experience which is so close to the super-natural. In one way or another all of these unhappy persons relate their sufferings to things in heaven and earth not dreamt of in our philosophy. As the modern view has emerged of Hawthorne as realistic and even sardonic, we incline to find in his writings a half-sarcastic condescension toward man's wishful belief in a divine interference in his affairs. Certainly he seems to echo, with the implication of a negative answer, Cotton Mather's oft-repeated query: "What can I see of the glo-rious God in these occurrences?" From his comments upon his own tribulations, and indirectly from the novels and tales, we know that he thought living a basically grim business. . . .

The Scarlet Letter was published in the spring of 1850, and in August Hawthorne moved to the "Red House" in Lenox, Massachusetts. He was now forty-six years old. Though weari-ness from his supreme intellectual effort and sadness from the death of his mother in the preceding year had induced a low-ered tone of body and mind, he was revived by the almost immediate recognition of his novel. "Mr. Fields tells me," he set down in his notebook May 5, 1850, "that two publishers in London had advertised *The Scarlet Letter* as in press." Yet so deeply had he drawn upon his inner strength that a revulsion of feeling came over him toward the book itself.

Before him lay the most active literary period of his career, as well as his seminal friendship with Herman Melville. If we include *A Wonder-Book for Girls and Boys* (1851) and his cam-paign biography, the *Life of Franklin Pierce* (1852), he was to publish, before his appointment in the following year to the Liverpool consulate, no fewer than five volumes [including] *The House of the Seven Gables* (1851) and *The Blithedale Romance* (1852). . . .

ART CREATED OUT OF MIND AND IMAGINATION

In the end, our study of Hawthorne leaves us with an abiding sense of the integrity of his mind and art. Few American writ-

ers have obeyed so implicitly as he the imperious, unconscious dictates of genius. In him dwelt no impatience for effect,
no diversion to extraneous themes, either by emulation of
other writers or by the pressures of the stormy world just outside Salem and Concord; he never strained beyond himself.
From the writing of his first sketches until *The Dolliver
Romance* his art, however narrow, remained supremely natural, without pretense, defying imitation. In the center of his
being, deeper even than his passion for perfect expression, lay
a microcosm of the New England Puritan mind; its ways of
thought were integuments [outer coverings] of himself.
Indeed, he had never needed to learn how the Puritan mind
worked, for to him by the time he had written *Twice-Told Tales*
the revelation of its meaning was complete. . . . His was a res-
olute fulfillment of private artistic principles.

Yet in the America of the nineteenth century, Hawthorne's
consecration [devotion] to artistic purposes was not an
uncommon experience. Those who live in the desert must find
in their own souls secret springs. Some of our most powerful
writers have been those who looked intensely within at the
spiritual experiences induced by their very isolation. So
Emerson himself as he walked through the snow puddles of
Boston Common was "glad to the brink of fear"; and so
[American poet] Emily Dickinson in the brick house on the
village street fell in love with Eternity—and described it, too.
Possibly, then, it was Hawthorne's poverty which begot his
riches. In the Puritan experience, so austere that it still moved
men to fear or anger, he discovered, with his artist's eyes
turned inward, the enduring fabric of art.

The Social Criticism of a Public Man

Sculley Bradley, Richmond Croom Beatty,
and E. Hudson Long

Many biographers present Nathaniel Hawthorne's solitude as a somber time, but Sculley Bradley, Richmond
Croom Beatty, and E. Hudson Long present a different
view. Though Hawthorne deliberately chose to study
writing and Puritanism, tasks he could only do alone,
they argue that otherwise, he was a public man, living
with and observing his fellow New Englanders or performing his duties as a foreign consul. His interest in
the lives of his fellow humans led him to examine the
relationship between the individual and society. Guilt,
Hawthorne concluded, corrodes lives, and nature and
freedom from guilt brings "sweetness."

To understand Hawthorne the reader must set aside an attractive legend. Only accidental circumstances support the tradition of the shy recluse, brooding in solitude upon the gloomi-
er aspects of Puritan New England whose writings are a kind
of spiritual autobiography. Instead, during most of his life,
Hawthorne was decidedly a public figure, capable, when necessary, of a certain urbanity. As a writer he set out quite consciously to exploit his antiquarian enthusiasms and his
understanding of the colonial history of New England. He was
absorbed by the enigmas of evil and of moral responsibility,
interwoven with man's destiny in nature and in eternity; but
in this interest he was not unusual, for he shared it with such
contemporaries as [Edgar Allan] Poe, [Ralph Waldo] Emerson,
and [Herman] Melville, and with others more remote, such as
[John] Milton and [William] Shakespeare.

It is true that for some years after his graduation from college he lived quietly in quiet Salem, but a young man
engrossed in historical study and in learning the writer's craft

Excerpted from *The American Tradition in Literature*, edited by Sculley Bradley,
Richmond Croom Beatty, and E. Hudson Long, 3rd ed. Copyright ©1967, 1962, 1961,
1957, 1956 by W. W. Norton & Company, Inc. Courtesy of W. W. Norton & Company, Inc.

PURITAN MORAL LESSONS

*Puritan preoccupation with doing good and overcoming evil
prompted leaders to write tracts and books to guide citizens to
fulfill their moral duties. In* Essays to Do Good, *which was first
published in 1710, Cotton Mather, a Puritan minister and
writer, exhorts readers to remedy the ills brought on everywhere by mankind's sinful nature. An excerpt from the essay
"Much Occasion for Doing Good" reveals the moral tone that
Hawthorne thought caused a "corrosive sense of guilt."*

If men would set themselves to devise good, a world of good
might be done more than is now done, in this "present evil
world." Much is requisite to be done that the great God and
his Christ may be more known and served in the world; and
that the errors which prevent men from glorifying their
Creator and Redeemer may be rectified. Much is necessary to
be done that the evil manners of the world, by which men are
drowned in perdition [eternal damnation], may be reformed;
and mankind rescued from the epidemical corruption which
has overwhelmed it. Much must be done that the miseries of
the world may have suitable remedies provided for them; and
that the wretched may be relieved and comforted. The world
contains, it is supposed, about a thousand millions of inhabitants. What an ample field do these afford, for doing good? In
a word, the kingdom of God in the world calls for innumer-
able services from us. To do such things is to do good.

Cotton Mather, *Essays to Do Good,* in *The American Tradition in Literature,*
edited by Sculley Bradley, Richmond Croom Beatty, and E. Hudson Long. 3rd
ed. Vol. 1. New York: W. W. Norton, 1967.

is not notably queer [eccentric] if he does not seek society or
marriage, especially if he is poor. In later years Hawthorne
successfully managed his official duties, made a large circle of
friends, and performed the extrovert functions of a foreign
consul with competence, if without joy. . . .

The twelve years of so-called "seclusion" in his mother's
Salem home were years of literary apprenticeship. He read
widely, preparing himself to be the chronicler of the antiquities
and the spiritual temper of colonial New England. . . . He made
observant walking trips about Massachusetts; remote portions
of New England he frequently visited as the guest of his uncle,
whose extensive stage-coach business provided the means. . . .

AN OUTWARD LOOK AT LIFE'S DEEPEST PROBLEMS

Although in many of his stories, and in the two great novels
[*The Scarlet Letter* and *The House of the Seven Gables*], Haw-

thorne created genuine characters and situations, he holds his permanent audience primarily by the interest and the consistent vitality of his criticism of life. Beyond his remarkable sense of the past, which gives a genuine ring to the historical reconstructions, beyond his precise and simple style, which is in the great tradition of familiar narrative, the principal appeal of his work is in the quality of its allegory, always richly ambivalent, providing enigmas which each reader solves in his own terms.

Reference is made to his discovery of the Puritan past of his family, the persecutors of Quakers and "witches"; but wherever his interest started, it led him to a long investigation of the problems of moral and social responsibility. His enemies are intolerance, the hypocrisy that hides the common sin, and the greed that refuses to share joy.

He fears beyond everything withdrawal from mankind, the cynical suspicion, the arrogant perfectionism that cannot bide its mortal time—whatever divorces the pride-ridden intellect from the common heart of humanity. It is not enough to call him the critic of the Puritan; the Quaker or the transcendental extremist might be equally guilty; and [the characters] Wakefield, Aylmer, and Ethan Brand are not Puritans. His remedy is in nature and in the sweetness of a world freed not from sin, but from the corrosive sense of guilt.

Hawthorne Ranks High Among American Authors

Jay B. Hubbell

Jay B. Hubbell's survey of opinion of Nathaniel Hawthorne includes Hawthorne's contemporaries as well as modern scholars. Though his contemporaries praised him, Hawthorne had a humble attitude toward his work. Publishers and reviewers enthusiastically predicted Hawthorne's success if he would abandon anonymous publication, and shepherded *The Scarlet Letter* from sketch to full-length work. Fellow writers Edgar Allan Poe and Herman Melville promoted his reputation and referred to his qualities of genius. Yet, Hawthorne, who liked to hike the country trails, feared that only the path he trod would remember him, according to Ralph Waldo Emerson's 1865 journal. After Hawthorne's death in 1864, British writer Matthew Arnold said that "his literary talent is of the first order." And in 1949 scholars of American literature ranked him in first place among American authors.

Nathaniel Hawthorne (1804–1864), now rated as one of our three or four greatest writers, was for a dozen years or more, as he phrased it, "the obscurest man of letters in America." That misfortune was due in part to his lack of that business acumen which many popular authors seem to possess. Year after year he was publishing his fine stories and essays in gift-books and annuals but never over his own name or even a single pseudonym. A journalist and minor poet, Park Benjamin, who knew Hawthorne, in October, 1836, reviewed in the *American Monthly Magazine* a volume of the *Token* which contained no less than three pieces from Hawthorne's hand, not one of them signed with his own name. Benjamin gave

From Jay B. Hubbell, "Six Major Writers of the American Renaissance," in *Who Are the Major American Writers?*, pp. 39-42. Durham, NC: Duke University Press, 1972. Reprinted with permission.

this shrewd advice to the modest author: "If Mr. Hawthorne would but collect his various tales and essays into one volume, we can assure him that their success would be brilliant—certainly in England, perhaps in this country." Hawthorne did in the following year bring out the first edition of *Twice-Told Tales*. Without his knowledge a college friend, Horatio Bridge, had guaranteed the publisher against loss. Another college classmate, [Henry Wadsworth] Longfellow, reviewed the book in the *North American Review*.

A second edition of *Twice-Told Tales* in 1842 attracted the attention of Edgar Allan Poe, who as editor of *Graham's Magazine* was in a position to promote Hawthorne's reputation. Poe found in the tales "invention, creation, imagination, originality." His fascination with Hawthorne led him to write "The Oval Portrait," which clearly reveals Hawthorne's influence. In August, 1844, Poe wrote to [James Russell] Lowell: "He [Hawthorne] is a man of rare genius.". . .

HAWTHORNE'S MODESTY AMID GROWING FAME

It was [Herman] Melville's reading of *Mosses from an Old Manse* in 1850 that led him to write the panegyric [a public compliment] which he entitled "Hawthorne and His Mosses." After the publication of *The Scarlet Letter*, Melville wrote to [anthologist and editor] Evert Duyckinck on February 12, 1851, that he regarded Hawthorne "as evincing a quality of genius, immensely loftier, & more profound, too, than any other American has shown hitherto in the printed form. [Washington] Irving is a grasshopper to him—putting the souls of the two men together, I mean." Without "the shock of recognition" that came to him from his relations with Hawthorne, Melville might never have written such a masterpiece as *Moby-Dick*.

Hawthorne's first mature novel, *The Scarlet Letter*, was a best-seller. For that popular success some of the credit must go to his friend James T. Fields of the firm of Ticknor and Fields. Hawthorne had long hoped to publish a novel, but he was still only a writer of tales when Fields visited him in Salem one cold winter day and took back to Boston "the germ" of *The Scarlet Letter*. In Hawthorne's plan that story was merely the longest in a new volume of tales which he planned to call "Old-Time Legends; Together with Sketches, Experimental and Ideal." That title, as [critic and poet] George E. Woodberry remarked in his life of Hawthorne, is "fairly ghostly with the transcendental nonage of his genius, pale, abstract, ineffectual, with oblivion lurking in every syllable. Fields knew better than that." It was Fields who persuaded the doubting tale-writer to expand the long story into a novelette and to leave out the other tales that he had planned to include. Toward the end of his life Hawthorne wrote to Fields: "My literary success, whatever it has been, or may be, is the result of my connection with you."

ADMIRING CALLERS

Nathaniel Hawthorne was the object of awe and praise from ordinary citizens who visited his home in Lenox, Massachusetts, where he moved his family shortly after The Scarlet Letter *was published. Biographer Randall Stewart describes the Hawthornes' reactions to two unexpected callers.*

Lenox was a sociable place, and the Hawthornes especially enjoyed the social expansiveness after the morgue-like atmosphere of old Salem. "It is very singular," Sophia remarked, "how much more we are in the center of society in Lenox than we were in Salem." Except for the years abroad, the Hawthornes never saw so many people or experienced so much social activity. Berkshire was already a fashionable summer resort; it was also something of a literary community, in which Hawthorne, now famous, could hardly avoid conspicuousness.

Many callers were strangers who wanted to see the author of *The Scarlet Letter* and, in some cases, the letter itself. A Miss Phelps of New York, whose face seemed hard and pitiless to Sophia, stopped to have a look at the great writer. Sophia noted how she "devoured" Hawthorne with her eyes, and was shocked further at the lady's boldness in calling Julian "superb" in one breath and in the next "the image of his father"—all being, no doubt, a distressing example of New York manners. A more agreeable admirer was Elizabeth Lloyd, a friend of [poet John Greenleaf] Whittier's, whose visit Hawthorne recorded in "Twenty Days." "She had a pleasant smile," he wrote, "and eyes that readily responded to one's thought; so that it was not difficult to talk with her;—a singular, but yet a gentle freedom in expressing her own opinions;—an entire absence of affectation. . . . She did not bore me with laudations of my own writings, but merely said that there are some authors with whom we felt ourselves privileged to be acquainted, by the nature of our sympathy with their writings." So delighted was Hawthorne with Miss Lloyd that he declared her visit the only pleasant one he had thus far experienced in his capacity as author.

Randall Stewart, *Nathaniel Hawthorne: A Biography*. New Haven, CT: Yale University Press, 1948.

Hawthorne was a modest man who was never sure that any of his books would meet with the favor of the reading public. In the memorable passage which Emerson wrote in his *Journals* just after Hawthorne's death in 1864, we find this sentence: "One day, when I found him on the top of his hill, in the woods, he paced back the path to his house, and said, *'This path is the only remembrance of me that will remain.'*"

HAWTHORNE'S FAME SPREADS ABROAD

After the publication of *The Scarlet Letter*, as [critic] Clarence Gohdes has noted, "approval of Hawthorne was all but universal in British critical circles," and at the end of the century he was regarded as among American writers "the leading artist." In his discourse on Emerson in 1883 [British writer] Matthew Arnold confessed that Hawthorne's subjects were not for him "subjects of the highest interest; but," he added, "his literary talent is of the first order, the finest, I think, which America has yet produced,—finer, by much, than Emerson's."

When [British editor] John Morley asked Henry James to write a biography of Hawthorne for the English Men of Letters series, there was no American writer among the twenty-nine authors included in it. Published in 1879, the little book contains some admirable criticism. It is in fact the first book-length critical study of an American writer. James, however, had only recently come to his momentous decision to live and write in Europe rather than in the United States, and in *Hawthorne* he harped too much on the provincialism of New England and the barrenness of literary material in American life. The chief faults that he found in Hawthorne's masterpiece, *The Scarlet Letter*, were "a want of reality and an abuse of the fanciful element, a certain superficial symbolism." Poe before James, and [critic] W. C. Brownell after him, were also to condemn Hawthorne's excessive fondness for symbolism. There is, however, no mistaking James's admiration for the novelist who taught him that an American writer could be an artist. In the concluding paragraph of the book James wrote: "He was a beautiful, natural, original genius. . . . His work will remain; it is too original and exquisite to pass away. . . . No one has had just that vision of life, and no one has had a literary form that more successfully expressed his vision."

MODERN CRITICS VIEW HAWTHORNE

In the 110-odd years since these words were written few competent critics have denied Hawthorne a place among our

greatest writers. [Critic and biographer] Allen Tate, for example, writing in his *Reactionary Essays* (1936) maintained that
the New England renaissance produced "two talents of the
first order—Hawthorne and Emily Dickinson." In the scholars'
poll of 1949 the twenty-six specialists in American literature
gave Hawthorne first place with a total of 164 points. Poe was
second with 163.

In his edition of *The English Notebooks* [editor and biogra-
pher] Randall Stewart wrote in 1941: "Out of the restored journals and letters a new Hawthorne will emerge: a more virile
and a more human Hawthorne; a more alert and (in a worldly sense) a more intelligent Hawthorne; a Hawthorne less
dreamy, and less aloof, than his biographers have represented
him as being." This is the new Hawthorne that appears in
Stewart's *Hawthorne: A Biography* (1948) and in the numerous books and articles that have marked the Hawthorne
revival. The varied critical tests and approaches that critics
have brought to bear upon his books have not resulted in any
appreciable diminution of his fame.

A Skeptic Incompatible with His Time and His Past

Henry Seidel Canby

Henry Seidel Canby argues that Nathaniel Hawthorne belonged neither to the developing industrial age nor to the Puritan past. Hawthorne saw the new machine age growing "like a fungus" and viewed the hope and optimism of transcendentalists with skepticism. Already he had rejected the Calvinist religious doctrine of his ancestors. Skeptical of both the present and the past, Hawthorne found themes for his art by choosing the subject of Puritan rigidity in which to explore the psychological effects of sin. According to Canby, Hawthorne's characters are failures, victims, and deluded people whose moral wrongs and mental anguishes seem trivial to many twentieth-century critics. Canby argues that the characters' responses to their wrongdoings are more important than the acts themselves. The effects of sin on his characters' minds and spirits is a recurring theme in Hawthorne's works.

Nathaniel Hawthorne was a mystery, even to himself, and, like [Herman] Melville, he has remained a man of mystery in American literature, whose heart successive biographers have tried to bare, each one with a different explanation. . . .

There is no great philosophic secret in the abyss of Hawthorne's nature. There is not even a mystery. He was not a mystic. He belongs with the artists who ask "How?" rather than with the philosophers who learn "Why?" His reticence comes from finding no solution to the problems that constantly beset him. His reserve and love of solitude were the defenses of an imagination formed by peculiar circumstances and playing upon circumstances still more peculiar. What

Excerpted from *Classic Americans: A Study of Eminent American Writers from Irving to Whitman* by Henry Seidel Canby (Russell & Russell, 1959).

profundity he has is by intuition, not by logic, and his success is the success of an imaginative dreamer (not a thinker) with a genius for looking backward at the very moment when the rest of his generation were absorbed in what was ahead. . . .

THE BREAKDOWN OF PURITANISM AND THE RISE OF INDUSTRIALISM

The Hawthorne I am trying to interpret saw the New England town in its first real decadence, a civilization breaking up. He saw all about him (and constantly records) the new machine industry, which on country streams and in mountain valleys was penetrating New England like a fungus growth, sapping the last vitality from farm life, but bringing a new and rapid prosperity. . . . But with Hawthorne it is disinterest that defines his attitude, not dislike. The mechanical age did not catch his attention except as it suggested figures for his symbolism. . . .

Reality for Hawthorne was moral reality, and it was the lack of a moral element in which he could believe that made his own times unreal to Hawthorne, and action in them, beyond the necessities of existence, futile. Still quainter to us than the old village, still further from practicable living as we know it, was the life governed by moral duty or devoted to a search for God that had been the ultimate reality of the Puritans. Against Puritanism as a theology and a system of ethics he was in life-long opposition. He had thrown over its Calvinism [religious beliefs based on John Calvin's doctrine that God is omnipotent and that salvation results from God's choice and God's grace] and he gave his best imagination to depicting the terrible results of its austerities. Yet, though he freed himself from its precepts, he never escaped from the brooding upon sin and the moral life that was the cause of Puritanism and its legacy.

It is impossible to comprehend Hawthorne without the Puritan background. Puritanism, for him, was a fortress from which he had escaped and was glad to be gone, and yet looked back to as a city fortified and strong in its certainties while he was a wanderer, clear-eyed, but uncertain and weak. The Puritan age and its sure morality was an obsession in his life. It was still the norm from which deviations could be measured. If success for his contemporaries was measured by action, and his failure to be interested in action depressed him, his real concern was with ideals diametrically different. They were the ideals, though not the fact, of Puritanism. Spiritual failures, moral failures, were for him, as for the Puritans, the great theme, and his great characters can all of them be described in no other terms. Calvinism had broken down, but the world for Hawthorne remained nevertheless a moral world, in which the new energies of industrialism were exactly equivalent to the commercialism of earlier ages. . . .

HAWTHORNE SKEPTICAL OF CALVINISM

Nathaniel Hawthorne rejected the harsh Calvinism of the Puritan past, and he doubted the optimism of his transcendentalist contemporaries. An excerpt from "Sinners in the Hands of an Angry God," a sermon by revivalist Jonathan Edwards, illustrates the sternness that Hawthorne rejected.

The God that holds you over the pit of hell, much as one holds a spider, or some loathsome insect, over the fire, abhors you, and is dreadfully provoked; His wrath towards you burns like fire; He looks upon you as worthy of nothing else, but to be cast into the fire; He is of purer eyes than to bear to have you in His sight; you are ten thousand times so abominable in His eyes, as the most hateful and venomous serpent is in ours. You have offended him infinitely more than ever a stubborn rebel did his prince. And yet, it is nothing but His hand that holds you from falling into the fire every moment. It is ascribed to nothing else, that you did not go to hell the last night; that you was suffered to awake again in this world, after you closed your eyes to sleep. And there is no other reason to be given why you have not dropped into hell since you arose in the morning, but that God's hand has held you up. There is no other reason to be given why you have not gone to hell, since you have sat here in the house of God, provoking His pure eyes by your sinful wicked manner of attending His solemn worship: yea, there is nothing else that is to be given as a reason why you do not this very moment drop down into hell.

O sinner! consider the fearful danger you are in: it is a great furnace of wrath, a wide and bottomless pit, full of the fire of wrath, that you are held over in the hand of that God, whose wrath is provoked and incensed as much against you, as against many of the damned in hell. You hang by a slender thread, with the flames of divine wrath flashing about it, and ready every moment to singe it, and burn it asunder.

Norman Foerster et al., eds., *American Poetry and Prose.* 5th ed. Vol 1. Boston: Houghton Mifflin, 1970.

Hawthorne was untouched by the new births of modernism about him, except for the natural depression of a man who cannot think with his neighbors. The decay of the old world excited him where the grossness of the new merely inspired distaste. He saw in the breakdown of Puritanism moral issues that had some aspects of eternity, but in the upbuilding of a new economic state, none that seemed to him significant.

Transcendentalism, of course, that refinement of spiritual unrest which filled New England and the New England West with a cloud of "seekers," "come-outers," and enthusiasts, could not fail to attract him, but only because of the companionship with fine minds it promised him, not for any hope in its doctrine. Through his own and his wife's friends he entered that circle of the rebellious who were opposed, like him, to the materialism of the new industrial age; Emerson interested him, Margaret Fuller fascinated him, Thoreau got his admiration—but Transcendentalism as such touched him not at all. It could not arouse him, for enthusiasm and optimism were both foreign to his nature, and the fact of moral disorder and decay stirred his imagination where the possibility of moral regeneration by pulling on mental boot straps left him cold. Ways of reform did not interest his skeptic nature, ideas for a future society could not hold his attention long, because he had the novelist's, not the philosopher's, eye, and human failures and their causes were more interesting to him than prophecies of success, one might truly say than success itself. Margaret Fuller's transcendental heifer that kicked over the milk pail at Brook Farm was his symbol for the rebellion of these intellectualists. He did not expect to escape from the "chaos" of time by the transcendental route. He was not, I think, really interested in escape, except in moods of financial discouragement. . . .

HAWTHORNE'S INTEREST IN SOCIETY'S FAILURES

The actual moral world seemed to him the business of the moment—the unfinished business, if you please, of a dying Puritanism. And in the moral world it is the failures, complete or qualified, that a novelist finds most interesting, and a novelist like Hawthorne, brooding upon the breakdown of a great system, would inevitably choose for his themes. . . . If Hawthorne had not been skeptical of Transcendentalism [a literary and philosophical movement associated with Ralph Waldo Emerson that asserted that an ideal spiritual reality exists and can be known by intuition], he would have turned away in any case the instant he began to write. For his mind was set on truth, not hope, and truth for every man resides only where he most feels reality.

And hence, in the feverish activity of the [1840s] and the [1850s], and in the felt presence of that unrivaled optimism which was already stirring [poet Walt] Whitman to paeans of democracy, Hawthorne chose for his characters the weak or the wounded from the great battlefields of Puritanism, or the dreamers and the self-deluded who wandered vainly in search of a new security. Is it necessary to specify, to name the personnel of *The Blithedale Romance, The Marble Faun, Septimius, The Scarlet Letter*, the short stories? They are all moral failures, whether victims, like Donatello, Hester, Ethan Brand, Hilda, or would-be conquerors, like Hollingsworth, Zenobia, Septimius, who are too often self-deceived. They belong one and all to a world of moral speculation in its last orbit, already eclipsed by industrialism, and to be darkened forever in New England. . . .

HAWTHORNE DOUBTS TRANSCENDENTALISM

An excerpt from essayist Henry David Thoreau's Walden *illustrates the transcendentalists' optimism, which Hawthorne also doubted.*

We must learn to reawaken and keep ourselves awake, not by mechanical aids, but by an infinite expectation of the dawn, which does not forsake us in our soundest sleep. I know of no more encouraging fact than the unquestionable ability of man to elevate his life by a conscious endeavor. It is something to be able to paint a particular picture, or to carve a statue, and so to make a few objects beautiful; but it is far more glorious to carve and paint the very atmosphere and medium through which we look, which morally we can do. To affect the quality of the day, that is the highest of arts. Every man is tasked to make his life, even in its details, worthy of the contemplation of his most elevated and critical hour.

Norman Foerster et al., eds., *American Poetry and Prose.* 5th ed. Vol 1. Boston: Houghton Mifflin, 1970.

Think of Hawthorne, then, as a man conditioned by Puritanism, though quite free from its theology and skeptical of its ethical code. Think of him as an observer set at the very moment when the sense of sin and the will to moral perfection alike give place to a justification by material success. Think of him as a skeptic among his fellow idealists who sees that the present is rushing on and away from the place of conflict where the secret of human destiny seemed about to be revealed and [who] turns backward brooding on the wreckage of the past, finding more to engage him in broken wills and frustrated hopes than in prosperity, and more wisdom in failure than in rosy Emersonian hope. Grant this, as one must, and it becomes easier to explain his broodings, his seclusion, his increasing maladjustment to life; and also his rather astounding success as an artist, a success caught at the very edge of failure. Here is to be found the reason why this gifted observer with "something of the hawk-eye" about him, turned instinctively to the methods of romance.

HAWTHORNE, THE TRUE SKEPTIC

For this success his skepticism was largely responsible, more so, I think, than his susceptibility to the romantic movement, which after all only gave him his opportunity. With [Herman] Melville and [Mark] Twain, he is one of the three great skeptics in American literature. . . . But Hawthorne was a true, a congenital, skeptic, who kept his heart in security no matter how wildly it throbbed, and never let his obsessive interest in the moral problems of humanity deceive him into certainty.

He was a skeptic of Puritanism, inevitably. He knew its annals, bore them in his own heredity. He had broken from its creed with his generation, even though he never escaped from the problems it had tried to solve by *force majeure*. The New England world was one pattern for him, dim in the distant past, sharp in the background, raveling into tatters at his feet, but woven through with the same themes of sin and grace and will. He did not believe in the Calvinistic dogma, and therefore could see it objectively from its source in the secret springs of error to its widespread and powerful effects. . . .

He was skeptical of the new economic world where science was to right all ills, but skeptical with the mild interest of a man who looks upon what does not concern him. . . . He was too skeptical of the values of industrialism to be dazed or angered by its confusions. The human problems resulting, about which one could not be skeptical, were all that really aroused his fascinated concern.

Skeptical of all cures, indifferent to what was itself an increasing indifference to the moral problems, he kept his head and his heart, and while others prepared for the Civil War and the physical development of the seventies, and Christian Science, and the triumph of mechanism, he went his own way and, like the captain of a derelict ship, made observations of the sun, the stars, the currents, eternal verities independent of time and taste.

To speak in plainer English, it was the thing itself—character, human nature, the soul—that interested Hawthorne, not tendencies, reconstructions, theories, and hopes. And when the dull soullessness of the immediate present of commercialism repelled him, and his transcendental friends' obstinate pursuit of their dreams left him cold, he turned backward in his brooding to the New England past (so close to his childhood) and found there one of the great treasure houses of human experience, a civilization characteristic and unique, built upon moral ideas that he understood to the core of his being, powerful with a dogmatism worth wrestling with, and illustrating in a thousand fashions those frailties of human certitude which skeptics love to brood upon; furthermore, a civilization rich for the artist in dramatic conflicts between the good will and sin. . . .

REALISM AND ROMANTICISM IN HAWTHORNE'S WORK

He was capable of realism, although he used it only to give names and local habitations to his moral imaginings. But realism alone would not serve his skeptical purposes. It is true that skepticism is antiromantic, and indeed, while Hawthorne's methods are borrowed from the romantic fashions of the day, I cannot see anything essentially romantic [characterized by interest in nature, imagination, and individual emotional expression] in his mind. Nor are the great passages in his best books romantic, if the term has any meaning beyond imaginative excellence. . . .

For Hawthorne, then, with his really profound insight into moral situations and his skeptic inability to solve them philosophically, or solve them at all (except by conventional punishments), romance was an obvious escape from intolerable difficulties in expression. The veil of unreality, the reticence of the indirect, the indefiniteness of fancy, which hold the interest yet never commit the writer to a final solution—these were tricks of the romanticist's trade ready at hand. . . .

Hawthorne himself was not content with his role of observer and felt that, in this respect, he was a frustrated man. He desired (like all the Concord men) to see through the mystery, and the best he could do was to record the failure of men and women to solve their problems, in stories which he felt (quite rightly) that his Puritan ancestors would have regarded as trivial. And to make his unsolved problems interesting, to express them at all as problems without committing himself to an answer, he had to charge and overcharge them with romance.

Indeed, as I have said, all of Hawthorne's best books are stories of failures. Couples, like the daguerreotypist [one using early methods of photography] and Phoebe in *The House of the*

Seven Gables, or Kenyon and Hilda, escape, but to a rather tame and uncertain future. The great figures—Hester, Dimmesdale, Zenobia, Miriam, Ethan Brand—all fail. And the books themselves are relative failures. In none of them, except perhaps in *The Scarlet Letter,* does Hawthorne blend in one luminous whole both the significance and the reality of the life he depicts, as [Russian writer Fyodor] Dostoevsky, [British novelist Thomas] Hardy, even [British novelist Henry] Fielding, all have done. He is always driven back (flies back would be a more accurate figure) to his romantic symbolism, which is left to be read in two or three possible ways. . . .

MODERN CRITICS MOCK HIS THEMES, BUT PRAISE HIS STYLE

This irreverent generation [of the 1950s] has mocked at Hawthorne's struggling souls who torture themselves over peccadillos like adultery and are morally wrecked by obsessions that (so it is assumed) any good psychoanalyst could remove. Studies in nerves seem to us more important than studies in morals, and certainly we are right in supposing that common sense and a working knowledge of science would have prevented half the casualties of literature. Hawthorne might retort by saying that without a moral sense you have of course no moral tragedies, and an observer of both epochs might add that the value of his literary psychology lies not in the deeds analyzed but in the picture of a struggle between right and wrong where the state of mind of the characters in conflict is immensely significant without regard to the rightness of what they think right or the wrongness of what they think wrong. If the plan of action seems great, not petty, that itself is an argument for the importance of the literary picture.

And indeed there is a lack of consistence between the scorn that our younger critics shower upon Hawthorne's moral creations and their respect for his style. They admit a dignity in the expression that they will not allow to the thing expressed.

Hawthorne's style has a mellow beauty; it is sometimes dull, sometimes prim [proper, even prudish], but is never for an instant cheap, never, like our later American styles, deficient in tone and unity. It is a style with a patina that may or may not accord with current tastes, yet, as with [perhaps Charles Farrar] Browne, [a humorist who wrote under the pseudonym Artemus Ward], [British essayist Joseph] Addison, [British essayist Charles] Lamb, [American essayist Henry David] Thoreau, is undoubtedly a style. Such styles spring only from rich ground, long cultivated, and such a soil was

Hawthorne's. . . . His style is the fulfillment of a long culture, turning toward literature only at its close. That this culture was Puritan determined the quality of the soil from which his rhythm came, but its depth and richness was due to the almost hysterical intensity of this civilization, where both the rigors and the opportunities of a new country had packed time with significant incident. . . .

THE DIGNITY OF BOTH THEME AND STYLE

And much of Hawthorne's success as a stylist must come from the dignity of his themes. Holding back from the new life of America into which Whitman was to plunge with such exuberance, he kept his style, like himself, unsullied by the prosaic world of industrial revolution, and chose, for his reality, the workings of the moral will. You can scarcely praise his style and condemn his subjects. Even romantic themes that would have been absurd in lesser hands get dignity from his purpose. . . .

Every powerful age gets its expressive writer, and though it was in a transition between two ways of thinking about living, one moral, one materialistic, that Hawthorne, fortunately for his skeptical and observant genius, was born, he is another instance of this fact. As Shakespeare, the Renaissance man, gave feudalism its final lift into the imagination, so Hawthorne, the skeptic with a moral obsession, raised New England Puritanism—not the theory, but the practice and still more the results in mind and spirit—into art. This lies behind his style.

The Wisdom of Hawthorne's Blackness

Herman Melville

New Englanders who had read Nathaniel Hawthorne's stories before 1850 thought of him as a pleasant writer whose tales had little deeper meaning. Herman Melville, one of Hawthorne's contemporaries, sees a different Hawthorne. In reading Hawthorne's *Mosses from an Old Manse*, Melville detects a dark side, a mystical blackness, emanating from Hawthorne's soul. He compares it to the darkness in William Shakespeare, whose tragic characters express dark truths. The blackness is not a simple symbol for sin or evil in either author. Rather, it represents a quality more complex, more deeply lodged within the human psyche, and gives expression to the negative emotions—the anguish and despair—that humans are capable of experiencing. Though Melville admits that Hawthorne may fall short of Shakespeare's reputation, he recommends that his fellow countrymen acknowledge Hawthorne as an "excellent author." Melville made his observation of Hawthorne before reading *The Scarlet Letter*, which clearly exemplifies the blackness that Melville detected in *Mosses*.

Herman Melville and Nathaniel Hawthorne are considered to be the two major authors in early American literature. Of Melville's several novels, his masterpiece is *Moby-Dick*.

It is curious how a man may travel along a country road, and yet miss the grandest or sweetest of prospects by reason of an intervening hedge, so like all other hedges, as in no way to hint of the wide landscape beyond. So has it been with me concerning the enchanting landscape in the soul of this Hawthorne, this most excellent Man of Mosses. [Hawthorne's *Mosses from an Old Manse* was published in 1846. Melville read the collection

Excerpted from Herman Melville's anonymous review of *Mosses from an Old Manse* in the August 17, & 24, 1850, issues of *Literary World* magazine.

of tales and sketches in 1850 and wrote the review while living in Pittsfield, Massachusetts. It appeared anonymously in the New York *Literary World,* August 17, 24, 1850.] His Old Manse has been written now four years, but I never read it till a day or two since. I had seen it in the book-stores—heard of it often—even had it recommended to me by a tasteful friend, as a rare, quiet book, perhaps too deserving of popularity to be popular.

But it is the least part of genius that attracts admiration. Where Hawthorne is known, he seems to be deemed a pleasant writer, with a pleasant style,—a sequestered, harmless man, from whom any deep and weighty thing would hardly be anticipated;—a man who means no meanings. But there is no man, in whom humour and love, like mountain peaks, soar to such a rapt height as to receive the irradiations of the upper skies;—there is no man in whom humour and love are developed in that high form called genius; no such man can exist without also possessing, as the indispensable complement of these, a great, deep intellect, which drops down into the universe like a plummet.

For spite of all the Indian-summer sunlight on the hither side of Hawthorne's soul, the other side—like the dark half of the physical sphere—is shrouded in a blackness, ten times black. But this darkness but gives more effect to the ever-moving dawn, that forever advances through it, and circumnavigates his world. Whether Hawthorne has simply availed himself of this mystical blackness as a means to the wondrous effects he makes it to produce in his lights and shades; or whether there really lurks in him, perhaps unknown to himself, a touch of Puritanic gloom,—this, I cannot altogether tell. Certain it is, however, that this great power of blackness in him derives its force from its appeals to that Calvinistic sense of Innate Depravity and Original Sin, from whose visitations, in some shape or other, no deeply thinking mind is always and wholly free. For, in certain moods, no man can weigh this world without throwing in something, somehow like Original Sin, to strike the uneven balance.

At all events, perhaps no writer has ever wielded this terrific thought with greater terror than this same harmless Hawthorne. Still more: this black conceit pervades him through and through. You may be witched by his sunlight—transported by the bright gildings in the skies he builds over you; but there is the blackness of darkness beyond; and even his bright gildings but fringe and play upon the edges of thunderclouds. In one word, the world is mistaken in this Nathaniel Hawthorne. He himself must often have smiled at its absurd misconception of him. He is immeasurably deeper than the plummet of the mere critic. For it is not the brain that can test such a man; it is only the heart. You cannot come to know greatness by inspecting it; there is no glimpse to be caught of it, except by intuition; you need not ring it, you but touch it, and you find it is gold.

BLACKNESS IN SHAKESPEARE'S *KING LEAR*

The blackness Herman Melville attributes to Hawthorne can be found in the tragedy of King Lear. The elderly king divides his lands between two daughters who flatter and fool him, and he banishes his silent, loving daughter. Discovering the truth and facing his own error is a black moment for Lear, who fears he will go mad. The king's lines in act 2, scene 4 express his grief.

> But, for true need—
> You heavens, give me that patience, patience I need!
> You see me here, you gods, a poor old man,
> As full of grief as age, wretched in both;
> If it be you that stirs these daughters' hearts
> Against their father, fool me not so much
> To bear it tamely; touch me with noble anger,
> And let not women's weapons, water drops,
> Stain my man's cheeks! No, you unnatural hags!
> I will have such revenges on you both
> That all the world shall—I will do such things—
> What they are yet, I know not, but they shall be
> The terrors of the earth! You think I'll weep;
> No, I'll not weep.
> I have full cause of weeping, but this heart
> Shall break into a hundred thousand flaws [fragments]
> Or ere I'll weep. O fool, I shall go mad!

William Shakespeare, *King Lear*, in *Eight Great Tragedies*, edited by Sylvan Barnet, Morton Berman, and William Burto. New York: New American Library, 1957.

Now, it is that blackness in Hawthorne, of which I have spoken, that so fixes and fascinates me. It may be, nevertheless, that it is too largely developed in him. Perhaps he does not give us a ray of light for every shade of his dark. But however this may be, this blackness it is that furnishes the infinite obscure of his background,—that background, against which Shakespeare plays his grandest conceits, the things that have made for Shakespeare his loftiest but most circumscribed renown, as the profoundest of thinkers. . . . But it is those deep faraway things in him; those occasional flashings-forth of the intuitive Truth in him; those short, quick probings at the very axis of reality;—these are the things that make Shakespeare, Shakespeare. Through the mouths of the dark characters of Hamlet, Timon, Lear, and Iago, he craftily says, or sometimes insinuates the things which we feel to be so terrifically true, that it were all but madness for any good man, in his own proper character, to utter, or even hint of them. . . .

But if this view of the all-popular Shakespeare be seldom taken by his readers, and if very few who extol him have ever read him deeply, or perhaps, only have seen him on the tricky stage (which alone made, and is still making him, his mere mob renown)—if few men have time, or patience, or palate, for the spiritual truth as it is in that great genius—it is then no matter of surprise, that in a contemporaneous age, Nathaniel Hawthorne is a man as yet almost utterly mistaken among men. Here and there, in some quiet armchair in the noisy town, or some deep nook among the noiseless mountains, he may be appreciated for something of what he is. But unlike Shakespeare, who was forced to the contrary course by circumstances, Hawthorne (either from simple disinclination, or else from inaptitude) refrains from all the popularising noise and show of broad farce and blood-besmeared tragedy; content with the still, rich utterance of a great intellect in repose, and which sends few thoughts into circulation, except they be arterialised at his large warm lungs, and expanded in his honest heart. Nor need you fix upon that blackness in him, if it suit you not. Nor, indeed, will all readers discern it; for it is, mostly, insinuated to those who may best understand it, and account for it; it is not obtruded upon every one alike. . . .

And now, my countrymen, as an excellent author of your own flesh and blood—an unimitating, and, perhaps, in his way, an inimitable man—whom better can I commend to you, in the first place, than Nathaniel Hawthorne. He is one of the new, and far better generation of your writers. The smell of young beeches and hemlocks is upon him; your own broad prairies are in his soul; and if you travel away inland into his deep and noble nature, you will hear the far roar of his Niagara. Give not over to future generations the glad duty of acknowledging him for what he is. Take that joy to yourself, in your own generation; and so shall he feel those grateful impulses on him, that may possibly prompt him to the full flower of some still greater achievement in your eyes. And by confessing him you thereby confess others; you brace the whole brotherhood. For genius, all over the world, stands hand in hand, and one shock of recognition runs the whole circle round.

Hawthorne's Use of Mythology

Hugo McPherson

Generations of critics have sought to explain the symbolism and allegory of Nathaniel Hawthorne's work.
According to Hugo McPherson, two previously overlooked children's books, *A Wonder-Book for Girls and
Boys* and *Tanglewood Tales*, a retelling of twelve Greek
myths, provide insight into Hawthorne's use of mythological themes to construct his own personal myth.
Expressed through symbols and allegories, the myth is
present in all of his tales and novels. At the center of
the myth is the heart, which is divided between reason
and imagination. According to McPherson, images of
daylight, sun, money, and power represent reason;
images of night, the moon, fountains, mirrors, and
magic symbolize imagination. Like heroes in Greek
stories, Hawthorne's characters pursue a hero's quest,
but they can succeed only if they reconcile the opposites of reason and imagination.

The imaginative foundation of a writer's work may well be an
inner drama or 'hidden life' in which his deepest interests and
conflicts are transformed into images or characters; and
through the symbolic play of these creations, he comes to
'know' the meaning of his experience; the imaginative structure becomes a means of reaching truth. . . . The total creation
of the artist is not his written works but a living, interior
drama; he lives 'a life of allegory,' and each of his works
expresses one facet or another of the total structure. . . .

THE HEART AS HAWTHORNE'S LEADING SYMBOL

[The Heart became] Hawthorne's central preoccupation and
his leading symbol. Everything he has to say is related, finally, to 'that inward sphere.' For the Heart is the meeting place

Excerpted from *Hawthorne as Myth-Maker: A Study in Imagination* by Hugo McPherson;
© 1969 by the University of Toronto Press. Reprinted with permission of the University of
Toronto Press.

of all the forces—spiritual and physical, light and dark, that compete for dominance in man's nature. Criticism has dealt at great length with the Heart and its complexities, but Hawthorne's 'personal legend' reveals its centrality in a new way. Those who read him as a Christian moralist recognize instantly an opposition between Head and Heart, reason and passion which is related not only to Puritan theology but to the Neo-Classical view of man: 'Reason the card, but passion is the gale.' But to conclude that Hawthorne thinks of Reason as a presiding faculty which must restrain and direct the depraved Heart is to forget that he allied himself with the Romantics in regarding Imagination as the supreme instrument of vision. For Oberon-Hawthorne [Oberon is king of the fairies, source of magic], the realm of imagination is the realm of night, of moonlight and magic; it is in this realm that one truly 'sees.' Reason belongs in the daylight realm of empirical action, and is concerned with law, measurement, and mechanism; it is efficacious in getting the world's work done. Unquestionably the Head-Heart conflict was primary in the Puritan vision of man's experience, for Puritanism equated imagination not with Oberon's magic but with witchcraft and demonism. . . . In Hawthorne's personal vision, however, we have not a bipolar Head-Heart conflict but a tableau in which the Heart is central, flanked by two suitors—the empirical, daylight faculty of Reason and the nocturnal, magical power of Imagination. The Heart, then, far from being a sink of evil as Calvinism [religious beliefs based on John Calvin's doctrine that God is omnipotent and that salvation results from God's choice and God's grace] would have it, is for Hawthorne the characteristically human realm—as complex as the Cretan labyrinth [the maze that confined the Minotaur], sometimes as black as Hell itself; but though its 'gloom and terror may lie deep . . . deeper still is the eternal beauty,' [Hawthorne wrote in *The American Notebooks*, edited by Randall Stewart]. And when the Heart is touched by love, man discovers his true humanity. . . .

INSIGHT FOUND IN TWO CHILDREN'S BOOKS

But in what way does the personal myth inform his fiction? And what are the mythological situations that give his work coherence as an *oeuvre* [the complete body of a writer's work]? . . .

The mythological substructure of Hawthorne's work has not been clearly identified before now because criticism has neglected two of his simplest and apparently most inconsequential works, *A Wonder-Book for Girls and Boys*, and *Tangle-*

wood Tales—twelve episodes from Greek mythology which he retold for children. The literary merit of these tales is not great, although several of them persist in the imagination. . . . Their most striking feature for the critic, however, is that Hawthorne allowed himself to treat these 'immortal fables' as ideal forms created in 'the pure childhood of the world,' and justified his radical re-working of them on the ground that they were 'indestructible' and that 'the inner life of the legends cannot be come at [approached] save by making them entirely one's own property.' The result is a body of stories which in their purified state may make 'very capital reading' for children; but at a deeper level they constitute an 'ideal' myth which reveals Hawthorne's highest aspirations for the individual, the community, and the artist. This happy narrative, so striking in contrast to the dark tales of New England experience, provides the most direct access to the 'inward sphere' of Hawthorne's imagination.

Three themes dominate in Hawthorne's re-creation of the materials that he found in Charles Anthon's *Classical Dictionary* [of names in ancient Greek and Roman writings]. The first, as revealed in the legends of Perseus, Cadmus, Bellerophon, Jason, Theseus, and Hercules, is the narrative of the hero: a young man undertakes a dangerous quest; he undertakes it at the prompting, or command, of a jealous king, an uncle or father; its fulfillment involves the killing of a monster; and the hero's reward (with the exception of Hercules and Bellerophon, the rider of Pegasus) is kingship. A related narrative, the stories of Pandora, Circe, and Proserpina, deals with an attractive female who, like Eve, appears to be responsible in one way or another for mankind's fallen state [called the theme of the Dark Lady]. And the third situation, treated in the tales of Baucis and Philemon, Midas, and the Pygmies, underlines the ideas that man's happiness is inextricably involved with the happiness of his fellows; men must learn to be brothers. The pattern of a quest, however, is central, though it is not, finally, separable from the related themes of the Dark Lady and the brotherhood of man.

In Hawthorne's rendering of the hero's quest, the reader soon recognizes recurring images which characterize two sides of the hero's experience. The daylight world in which the quest begins is associated with sun, flame, money, iron, power, the senses, and the narrow rationalism of law; this is the empirical realm, the concrete dimension of man's temporal experience. The moonlit world which the hero enters is an insubstantial area where he will accomplish his mission 'as though in a dream'; it is associated with the air, invisibility, mirrors, fountains, and magic; this is the realm of imagination, the dusky area in which the hero discovers his power. . . .

THE HERO'S QUEST—A MYTH OF THE SELF

This central narrative of Hawthorne's, though given substance in dramatic personalities, is in one sense interior—a myth of the self. The hero's quest is an exploration of the menacing darkness of his own identity; it involves a long, night journey, as with Perseus and Cadmus, or the entry of a labyrinth or forest, as with Theseus and Jason. The hero's victory is the recognition and control of these forces, and the application of his new power to the problems of his community. Hawthorne underlines this dimension of the quest as a private 'initiation' when he remarks of the Cretan labyrinth: 'There can be nothing else so intricate, unless it were the brain of a man like Daedalus, who planned it, or the heart of any ordinary man.' Until this ordeal is past—until the forces of the darkest reaches of the self are brought under control—the hero cannot act creatively in the empirical world. The ideal end of the quest is the achievement of a new balance between the opposed forces of matter and spirit, sun and moon, reason and imagination. Then the hero can rule, and perhaps marry.

In this sense, Hawthorne's 'ideal' myth is optimistic in tone: each new generation of heroes brings back to the world of things an imaginative power which enables him to become a king—a benefactor of his race. . . . The hero, in short, may become a king, like Perseus, a city-builder, like Cadmus, or an artist, like Bellerophon. The myth expresses the ideals of the self, the community, and the artist. But this central narrative is not as simple as it appears, for there are a dozen other forces or personalities, active or passive, imaginative or materialistic, who aid or hinder the quest, and who may even make it miscarry. . . .

Before we turn from the ideal myth to Hawthorne's narratives of New England experience, however, we must consider the two related mythological situations mentioned above. The first might be called 'the brotherhood of man' theme. Again and again Hawthorne talks of 'unhumanized' hearts that have turned to iron, gold, marble, or stone. But the Heart's true elements are warm if fallible flesh and blood, and its presiding values should be sympathy and love. The Heart is the emblem of 'our common nature,' and until mankind recognizes and affirms its warm values he will fail equally in his social and individual quests. . . . Hawthorne believed that 'We must love one another or die.' The goal of the quest is the brotherhood of man, or in social terms the 'final triumph' of the republic; it will be reached not by reformers or builders but by a growth of self-awareness and vision.

THE CREATIVE DARK LADY

The second situation is far more complex. It is a feminine version of the hero's quest, revealed in the tales of Circe, Pandora, and Proserpina. The protagonist of this narrative is the Dark Lady who has so fascinated Hawthorne's readers and critics. To begin with, as her fecund charms indicate, she is primarily a creature of the empirical realm, but she is also a creative 'force.' Where the hero creates ideas or works of art, she creates babies, and this creative act is linked with the realm of night. Like the questing hero, she has had her dark initiation in the moonlit world. But for Hawthorne she is no more a figure of guilt than is the artist. The creative act, whether fiction or procreation, is fundamental to human nature; and man must accept his creativity rather than condemn it. . . .

In the ideal myth, then, the Dark Lady is blameless. It is only in the Christian tradition that she has become a figure of fear, haunted by the spectre of a Black Man [a devil] who will never let society forget that she knows the realm of night. Her Christian embodiments—Miriam [heroine in Hawthorne's *The Marble Faun*], Zenobia [a passionate and queenly woman in *The Blithedale Romance*], and Hester [the guilty woman in *The Scarlet Letter*]—detest the shadow which haunts them, but Calvinist men will never clear them of its opprobrium. The figure of the Dark Lady thus prepares us to enter the world of experience—the historical locale of Hawthorne's New England fiction.

For those, like Melville, who sensed the implications of Hawthorne's journey into the labyrinth of experience in America, his tales were sombre indeed. The Puritans had, with a breath-taking fortitude, gone on a long and perilous voyage from their tyrannical fatherland, and they were finally to escape its jealous power entirely. But their quest had somehow failed to produce the creative self-knowledge that crowned the adventures of Perseus and Bellerophon. Hawthorne saw them as men of iron and blazing sunlight, like the tyrants of the mythological tales—materialists who feared the night and the dark forests as the dwelling place of monstrous witches and demons. In the light of day they achieved triumphs of city-building, trade, and manufacturing, but Young Goodman Brown, as his name suggests, was their representative young hero—a Calvinist Everyman. The ambiguity of Brown's night journey suggests that his quest was the universal descent which all men must make into the depths of their own nature. But in contrast to the heroes of the ideal myth the outcome of Goodman Brown's quest is tragic. . . . And so Brown returns from the journey overshadowed by the thought that the night side of his nature, and of mankind's, is monstrous. This Puritan vision of evil blights his entire life, or at least makes it passive suffering, and even 'his dying hour was gloom.' In its very beginnings, then, the New England quest was in some degree abortive. The Puritans' legalistic, rationalistic, 'heartless' theology, as Hawthorne saw it, pre-doomed them to a kind of half-life. . . .

But if America's young heroes and heroic young America alike failed to achieve an ideal fulfillment of their quests, Calvinist theology was not entirely responsible, though it presented an initial difficulty. As Hawthorne turned from the terrors of Satan and the forest, he saw in every period of America's history promising heroes pursuing abortive quests which ended in isolation rather than in reconciliation of opposites and a new communion with their fellow men. The ultimate source of the failure was the denial of the values of the Heart—a denial often involuntary but nevertheless ending in cruel isolation. . . . Roger Chillingworth, the 'doctor' of *The Scarlet Letter*, ends as a fiend, for he uses his knowledge coldly and deliberately to torture and destroy Dimmesdale rather than to heal him. . . .

THE SCARLET LETTER AS AN AMERICAN MYTH

Hawthorne's first major analysis of the American situation was *The Scarlet Letter.* As Henry James perceived, Dimmesdale is—or should be—the hero of this narrative, although the story of the Dark Lady overshadows him. Today we would adjust this insight and describe him, in Northrop Frye's terms, as an 'ironic hero.' In Boston, Dimmesdale had achieved the highest place that the Puritan community accorded its men of vision—the pulpit; and from this eminence it was his duty to fight the powers of blackness. To the end of his career, Dimmesdale was a believing Calvinist, but his nature—even stronger than his belief—attracted him irresistibly to the lush, temporal charms of Hester, with whom he created a 'Pearl,' 'the union of their two natures,' and then, because of his faith, became an easy prey to the unending torture of guilt. By the same token, his Dark Lady, Hester, whose temporal creativity could scarcely, under the circumstances, be concealed, was persecuted by a community which feared both carnal knowledge and the mystery of creativity except as confined within the narrow limits set by religion and law.

To complicate this situation, the community unknowingly welcomed her husband, Roger Chillingworth, a deformed old scientist who had married Hester to warm the cold chamber of his heart, and who forces her to keep his identity a secret. In this repressive atmosphere he conveniently recalls 'his old faith' and becomes not a source of healing but a fiend who uses his knowledge of man's nature to torture the Puritan Dimmesdale to the point of death. But Hester privately refuses to accept the community's view of her nature as evil. Robbed of her real place in the town, she speculates boldly that human nature is naturally good. Finally, after meeting Dimmesdale on the scaffold at night and learning of his suffering, she refuses to keep Chillingworth's secret any longer, and in the 'natural' setting of the forest—as opposed to the legal forum of the marketplace—she offers Dimmesdale an escape to the wilderness or to Europe where she believes they can live by the law of their natures alone. For a moment Dimmesdale accepts, but then a flood of carnal images reveals to him that man's nature, unregulated by any law but instinct, is as unthinkable as the repressive Puritan scheme. His solution to the dilemma, therefore, is to confess his full nature publicly. Hester's power has given him strength to be an integrated man at last; God, he hopes, will be a merciful judge.

Dimmesdale's confession of his full nature 'humanizes' his daughter Pearl. She is a complete person, even though the Puritans regard her as a demon. But Pearl cannot survive in New England. . . . She escapes to Europe, endowed with Chillingworth's wealth—the chief 'good' that the Puritans produced. But, despite Dimmesdale's tragic death, the New England quest is not a complete failure, for Hester, the innocent Eve, finally returns to New England. Having hated her oppressors 'through seven long years,' she now repents of her unyielding pride and convinces them through gentleness and good works that she is not a temptress or witch but a nurse and benefactress. The Puritan austerity may be wrong, but man's imperfect nature must be governed. Man's full nature—its pearl—she believes, will yet be accepted in America. And the blood-red emblem which Pearl personifies, the *A*, will in another age become a symbol of honour: 'at some brighter period . . . a new truth would be revealed, in order to establish the whole relation between man and woman on a surer ground of mutual happiness,' [Hawthorne recorded in his notebooks]. For the *A*, as its position over the heart suggests, is the sign of the self—of the warm red bloodstream which mingles gifts that should be used, and frailties that are better recognized and controlled than scourged.

THE HEART AS A CAVERN

In his notebook entry of June 1, 1842, Nathaniel Hawthorne described the heart as a cavern that can be entered. Within the next few years following this entry, the image appeared in several sketches and stories, among them "The Christmas Banquet" and "Rappaccini's Daughter."

The human Heart to be allegorized as a cavern; at the entrance there is sunshine, and flowers growing about it. You step within, but a short distance, and begin to find yourself surrounded with a terrible gloom, and monsters of divers kinds; it seems like Hell itself. You are bewildered, and wander long without hope. At last a light strikes upon you. You peep towards it, and find yourself in a region that seems, in some sort, to reproduce the flowers and sunny beauty of the entrance, but all perfect. These are the depths of the heart, or of human nature, bright and peaceful; the gloom and terror may lie deep; but deeper still is the eternal beauty.

Nathaniel Hawthorne, *The American Notebooks.* Edited by Randall Stewart. New Haven, CT: Yale University Press, 1932.

So ended this New England quest. Dimmesdale, like Perseus, had found his identity, but only at the point of death. Hester, the Dark Lady, learned to accept her unhappy lot and await the bright revelations of such artists as Nathaniel Hawthorne. This gifted pair, at the price of great suffering, passed beyond the Puritan vision of evil. With the truth of man's nature revealed, the Black Man Chillingworth, with 'no more devil's work to do,' shrivelled and died.

Subsequent imaginative heroes (mercurial, moon types) would perhaps be more vigorous than Dimmesdale. But if they were to be more aggressive, their partners would have to be less aggressive than Hester, for in the world of Hawthorne's mythology two 'active' forces do not marry. Thus in the next romances Hawthorne's myth elaborated itself in an important new character, the pretty and fecund, but passive, maiden, a delightfully domestic creature who, like Cadmus's wife Harmonia, would be her husband's creative link with the empirical realm. . . . By the same token, the passive moon hero, the Dimmesdale of the first nineteen chapters of *The Scarlet Letter*, was to be perpetuated as a proper complement to the Dark Lady, although neither of this pair was to triumph in the new American community.

THE HOUSE OF THE SEVEN GABLES— AN AMERICAN QUEST NARRATIVE

Two centuries and seven long generations later, Hawthorne saw a happy fulfillment of the American quest in *The House of the Seven Gables*. This quest narrative involves a long struggle between two families: the imaginative craftsmen called Maule, the possessors of a beautiful piece of 'garden ground' with a clear, bubbling spring; and the Pyncheons, a family of Puritan materialists who regard the Maules as witches and steal their land as the site for a great house. In revenge, the Maules secrete the title to a great tract of 'Eastern land,' turn the clear well brackish, curse the sensual Pyncheons with something that resembles apoplexy, and return to torment them in dreams. Nevertheless, the Pyncheons triumph and the Maules disappear from view. In the course of seven generations, however, a more sympathetic strain of the Pyncheon family gains control of the house. Hepzibah, associated with owls—as Minerva is—and her brother Clifford, a Quicksilver type who has been banished to the darkness of a prison by the sun-tyrant Jaffrey, are in uncertain control of the house. This pair represent the frail and passive imagination of the nineteenth-century Puritans; unfortunately, they are too old and too weak to dominate their materialistic cousin Jaffrey. They give shelter, however, to a young couple, Holgrave and Phoebe. Holgrave is the last of the Maules, a vigorous and imaginative Daguerreotypist who 'makes pictures out of sunlight' in his dark chamber. Phoebe, far from reproducing the grasping materialism of her family, is a sunny, domestic angel. And this pair, the young moon hero and the cheerful young sun maiden, the last descendants of their lines, finally unite the warring families in a new and productive 'marriage.' Unlike his fore-bear who had attempted to enmesh Alice Pyncheon in the magic of wizardry, Holgrave captures Phoebe in 'love's web of sorcery.' The curse of the Maules carries off the hard-living Jaffrey, and the new inheritors of the Pyncheon-Maule property move to a new house, carrying their benign elders with them. Significantly, the new house will be built of wood. No family can build for its heirs; each generation must construct its own house. But what of the Eastern Land which the Anglophile Pyncheons hoped to wrest from the native Maules and exploit? Holgrave discovered its charter easily in the old house, and Clifford Pyncheon had known about it all along. He had thought of it as a vision—an ideal—which was not to be 'owned' by anyone, let alone the domineering Pyncheons. In the end, the Eastern Land turns out to be a thriving colony; it is the part of New England (or America) which the Puritans' greed failed to engulf.

The plot of *Seven Gables*, then, whatever its relation to fairy-tale or Gothic romance, is not the 'tiresome nuisance' that critics have complained of. Its outcome is an almost pastoral version of Hawthorne's central quest narrative, though the early events of the history are very dark comedy indeed; in sum, the action dramatizes with great subtlety the long quest of the nation's visionary powers to find their place of honour in the community, and to keep the Puritan ethos from dominating the entire Eastern Land. More important, perhaps, this perception of the informing principle of the romance reveals that all of Hawthorne's comments on the past—the advantages of frame houses, progress, and so forth—are relevant parts of the complete structure rather than tedious, 'tacked-on' morals. . . .

HAWTHORNE'S OEUVRE AS QUEST NARRATIVE

The 'principle of coherence' in Hawthorne's *oeuvre* [body of work] is a quest narrative—a myth in which the imaginative hero assumes that man can achieve happiness only in communion with his fellowmen; and that woman is not a slave of the Black Man but a creative complement to the hero—his point of contact with the material world. Because Hawthorne was an artist who saw clearly the phenomena of his social and intellectual tradition, he enriched this personal myth with a body of reflection and commentary that cannot be summarized at this stage of our investigation. . . . For the moment, one question remains: What is the relation of the informing myth to the vast body of criticism which has documented Hawthorne's theology, moral philosophy, political views, and so forth?

The present study, I think, does not run counter to such analyses, although it may place some of them in a new perspective. As his mythological tales make clear—and as a number of students of his thought have long since argued—the exact centre of his thought is the human heart, the *A*, the self. When empirical forces rule, as they do in the tyrants of Greek myth, or in the mechanical law of the Puritans, the rejected night side of the self may become monstrous or vengeful; it harasses the self with the wizardry of the Maules, the paralyzing gaze of the Gorgon Medusa, or the terrors of the Black Man and of witches. When imagination dominates, all is well; the community will progress to new heights. Evil, in these terms, is not to be explained; it is imperfection, the fundamental *donnée* [underlying assumption] of the human condition. And love is the force which redeems the mingled light and dark of the 'human realm.'

Given this basic view of experience, it becomes clear that, for Hawthorne, man's attempts to formulate schematically 'the one true system' are foreordained to failure. He could agree with [Ralph Waldo] Emerson that 'the law of my nature' should be recognized, but he could never agree that it must be followed undeviatingly, for unlike Emerson he believed that man's nature is imperfect. Hence, law and convention and ethical sanctions are a necessary part of life in society. But such laws and conventions should take into account the limitations of the men whom they govern. For these reasons, Hawthorne was a great democrat; he believed that, despite the self-aggrandizing motives of materialists, the interests of all men would finally triumph. Yet he scoffed at doctrinaire clergy, philanthropists, and reformers, including abolitionists. Like Emerson, he might have claimed: 'I have other slaves to free.' There would be no real abolition—no real end of man's inhumanity to man—until the realm of imagination achieved a place of authority in the affairs of the self, and hence of the community and the nation.

Finding a Voice in a New Nation

Peter Conn

After college, Nathaniel Hawthorne spent more than a decade reflecting on the nature of men and women and practicing the art of writing. When he emerged from that period, he needed a voice, an attitude, and a setting in order to express his spiritual feelings and insights. He joined the transcendentalists in their experiment in communal living on Brook Farm in Massachusetts, but, according to Peter Conn, he found neither the idealistic transcendentalists nor communal living compatible with his spirit. As a romantic, he wanted to look to the past, but America had but a short and thin history. For a time he lived in Rome, a city whose long history had shadows and mysteries. In the end, however, Conn writes, Hawthorne found in his own Puritan ancestors abundant material to give voice to tales and novels that explore the human condition.

Nathaniel Hawthorne was one of the original investors [in Brook Farm]; he committed fifteen hundred dollars to the project and moved to the [Massachusetts] farm in April 1841, shortly after it opened. Initially he took part enthusiastically, accepting more than his share of the community's barnyard tasks. "He is our prince," [Brook Farm organizer George] Ripley's wife wrote of him, "despising no labor, and very athletic and able-bodied." Disillusionment quickly followed; within seven months, Hawthorne had left Brook Farm. For the rest of his life, he referred to the episode as a romantic daydream.

Hawthorne's departure from Brook Farm was less surprising than his joining it in the first place. He was not disposed to submit to a communal regime. More seriously, his deepest views of life were not in accord with the buoyant transcendentalism upon which the experiment was based. He often insisted on the distance between himself and transcendentalist opinions. His experiences at Brook Farm itself provided some of the materials for his third novel, *The Blithedale Romance* (1852), an ironic assessment of the naive pretensions of the farm's inhabitants and, by implication, of all similar reformers. Earlier, in 1843, shortly after he left the farm, he published "The Celestial Railroad," which unmasks the defects of assorted liberal ideologies. In this story, transcendentalism is satirically personified as a fantastic giant, German by birth, indescribable even by his followers, an ill-proportioned heap of fog and duskiness. He fattens his disciples on meals of smoke, mist, moonshine, raw potatoes, and sawdust.

In fact, Hawthorne's response to the transcendentalists was more complex than this broad comedy would suggest. He was neighbor to most of the group, friend to some, and he acknowledged their cultural importance. In a paragraph affixed to the beginning of "Rappaccini's Daughter" (1844), he conceded that the transcendentalists "have their share in all the current literature of the world." Whatever his reservations, he was attracted by the moral earnestness of the transcendentalists and by their dissatisfaction with materialism and conventions. Like them, he was inquisitive about the intermixture of world and spirit, and he pondered the visible as a sign of the invisible.

ROMANTIC HAWTHORNE EYES THE PAST

At the same time, Hawthorne's romantic cast of mind was accompanied by an incorrigible irony that hung like a curtain between himself and his transcendentalist contemporaries. Unlike them, he was cautious about schemes for human perfection, and he was skeptical of any project that depended for success upon throwing off the burden of the past. The past had a far stronger hold on him than the future. His ancestral roots went back to the founding of Massachusetts, a heritage of two centuries that bore witness only to the ubiquity of human frailty. . . .

For Hawthorne, the past that his family and region shared was a moral tapestry interwoven of glory and shame, hope and decline. Against transcendentalist uplift, he harbored a fixed conviction that men and women would always be pulled backward and downward by the taint that lay like a canker within human nature. The lesson taught by history was inescapable, and he summarized it in the opening pages of *The Scarlet Letter*, as he recreated New England's earliest days: "The founders of a new colony, whatever Utopia of human virtue and happiness they might originally project, have invariably recognized it among their earliest practical necessities to allot a portion of the virgin soil as a cemetery, and another portion as the site of a prison." The cadence of the prose matches Hawthorne's sober theme. Hope is a delusion fit only for the innocent, and innocence, as Henry James would also see, is disabling and even dangerous.

CHORES ON BROOK FARM

Nathaniel Hawthorne, one of the original investors in the Brook Farm experiment in communal living, entered into its activities with enthusiasm. In an excerpt from his 1841 notebook, he tells about the farm work he did on April 14. Soon after, however, Hawthorne became disillusioned and left the project.

April 14th, 10 a.m.—. ... I did not milk the cows last night, because Mr. Ripley [one of the Brook Farm organizers] was afraid to trust them to my hands, or me to their horns, I know not which. But this morning I have done wonders. Before breakfast, I went out to the barn and began to chop hay for the cattle, and with such "righteous vehemence," as Mr. Ripley says, did I labor, that in the space of ten minutes I broke the machine. Then I brought wood and replenished the fires; and finally went down to breakfast, and ate up a huge mound of buckwheat cakes. After breakfast, Mr. Ripley put a four-pronged instrument into my hands, which he gave me to understand was called a pitchfork; and he and Mr. Farley being armed with similar weapons, we all three commenced a gallant attack upon a heap of manure. This office being concluded, and I having purified myself, I sit down to finish this letter. ...

Miss Fuller's cow hooks the other cows, and has made herself ruler of the herd, and behaves in a very tyrannical manner. ... I shall make an excellent husbandman,—I feel the original Adam reviving within me.

Nathaniel Hawthorne, *The American Notebooks*. Edited by Randall Stewart. New Haven, CT: Yale University Press, 1932.

Human limits lie like a smudge across the promise of felicity. With almost compulsive frequency, Hawthorne explored the dilemmas of men and women cut off from the "magnetic chain of humanity," isolated by circumstance or by choice. His most typical stories are darkly lyrical meditations on the devastating consequences that follow when love is withdrawn, whether because of egotism or prejudice or a failure of sexual nerve. In "The Minister's Black Veil," the Reverend Mr. Hooper inexplicably covers his face with an opaque cloth, becoming for the rest of his brief life an emblem of secret guilt and loveless despair. In "The Birthmark" and "Rappaccini's Daughter," men of science exchange human sympathy for a pernicious curiosity, ultimately murdering those they should love. In "Ethan Brand," the title character spends his life perversely seeking the unpardonable sin and finds it in the domination of humane feeling by manipulative intellect. Ethan Brand stands for all of Hawthorne's most malignant immoralists, a figure whose marble heart is merely an exotic symbol for the death of his human affections.

Almost all of Hawthorne's finest stories are remote in time or place. The glare of contemporary reality immobilized his imagination. He required shadows and half-light, and he sought a nervous equilibrium in ambiguity. Even his work that is set in the nineteenth century is usually marked by his characteristic preference for backward glances, for recovery and reconstruction. *The House of the Seven Gables* (1851) takes place in the Salem of Hawthorne's day, but the story's plot and the principal dramatic interest of the setting both depend upon the action of a seventeenth-century curse. Similarly, in *The Marble Faun* (1860), the present is overwhelmed by the long, lurid past of Rome. A history of ancient sin envelops the book like the malarial fogs that settled on the city each summer. It was this history that Hawthorne evoked in the preface to the novel, when he contrasted the rich fictional opportunities of Italy's centuries with the relative emptiness of America's raw democracy:

> Italy, as the site of his Romance, was chiefly valuable to him as affording a sort of poetic or fairy precinct, where actualities would not be so terribly insisted upon as they are, and must needs be, in America. No author, without a trial, can conceive of the difficulty of writing a romance about a country where there is no shadow, no antiquity, no mystery, no picturesque and gloomy wrong, nor anything but a common place prosperity, in broad and simple daylight, as is happily the case with my dear native land. It will be very long, I trust, before romance-writers may find congenial and easily handled themes, either in the annals of our stalwart republic, or in any characteristic and probable events of our individual lives. Romance and poetry, like ivy, lichens, and wall-flowers, need ruin to make them grow.

HAWTHORNE FINDS VOICE IN NEW ENGLAND PAST

The irony here is of course multiple. Hawthorne's complaints about his "dear native land" were familiar enough, and they would be echoed and repeated throughout the following decades. Painters and sculptors in some numbers, among them Robert W. Weir, Horatio Greenough, and Hiram Powers, set up studios in Italy for longer or shorter periods in order to root themselves in the tradition they could not discover at home. Hawthorne, however, despite his disclaimers, had long since discovered in the early history of his own New England the ruins and gloomy wrongs he found congenial. The elusive geography of romance, that landscape in which imagination and reality could collaborate in acts of transformation, had perhaps disappeared from the bustling commercial world of Jackson, Van Buren, and Pierce [American presidents between 1829 and 1857], but it remained accessible to the historical imagination.

The Puritan ancestors who provided Hawthorne with his amplest materials also gave him his angle of vision and instructed him in his technique. He once planned to call a group of his stories "Allegories of the Heart," and in that unused title he summed up much of his method and his subject. His chosen terrain lay between the realms of theology and psychology, and allegory provided the means of his explorations. Christianity as such had no appeal for him. Nonetheless, within a culture of religious crisis, from which traditional verities and their consolations had been dismissed, Hawthorne continued to feel the enduring relevance of spiritual evil as a subject for fictional inquiry. He felt as well the tug of explanations beyond the mundane and rational. He was a secularized Puritan symbolist, who recovered the dramas enacted in cases of conscience by tracing the lines that bound men and women to their motives. Concerned with individuals as specimens or types, he endowed his characters with solemnly stylized features and then studied their anxiety, or doubt, or guilt. He placed them amid settings and objects that gave symbolic expression to their inward states.

Where traditional allegory was secured in certitude, however, Hawthorne's allegorical proceedings yield only restlessness and doubt. The stable system of correspondences that tied allegory's images and ideas together was lodged squarely upon the religious orthodoxy that Hawthorne rejected. In his belated version of the sacramental world, the links binding visible to spirit have become vexed and problematic. Henry James wrote that he found in Hawthorne's work evidence of "the constant struggle which must have gone on between his shyness and his desire to know something of life; between what may be called his evasive and inquisitive tendencies." James's antitheses quite adroitly capture Hawthorne's peculiar version of allegory. The flickering, uncertain revelations offered by the physical world in Hawthorne's fiction allow simultaneously for confession and concealment, for discovery and disguise. This doubleness generates tensions that can be felt throughout Hawthorne's work, most memorably in his masterpiece, *The Scarlet Letter* (1850). The three great scaffold scenes that rise like spires in the architecture of the novel render fundamental human confrontations in which conflicting moral judgments find corollaries in contradictory views of reality itself. In the second of these scenes, Reverend Dimmesdale climbs the scaffold to confess his crime to an empty midnight square. The sky overhead is suddenly filled with the blaze of a meteor, whose intense, momentary glow lights the scene "with a singularity of aspect that seemed to give another moral interpretation to the things of this world than they had ever borne before." The alien grandeur of the scene confers a tragic nobility on the choices that Dimmesdale and Hester Prynne and Roger Chillingworth make. In the vanished New England of the seventeenth century, Hawthorne found the contrast and rebuke to the melancholy decay of his own generation.

He often chided himself for being an idler and mere scribbler. Though he never deserted his artistic allegiance, the looming specter of his grim, nation-building Puritan predecessors caused him to flinch apologetically from time to time. Furthermore, he was out of step with the prevailing entrepreneurial sentiments of his era, uneasy with what Henry James called the "genius of America." It was a genius, as James said dryly, that "has not, as a whole, been literary."

Hawthorne's Struggle with Method

Charles Feidelson Jr.

Nathaniel Hawthorne struggled with two questions concerning method: Should he portray the imaginative or the actual world? and, Should he write with symbolism or allegory? Charles Feidelson Jr. argues that Hawthorne never successfully resolved these dilemmas. In *The Scarlet Letter*, Hawthorne writes as a symbolist. In *The Marble Faun* and *The Blithedale Romance*, however, Hawthorne is neither a successful symbolist nor an effective allegorist. According to Feidelson, these unresolved issues weaken the novels.

Hawthorne had enormous respect for the material world and for common-sense reality; he admired the novels of [British novelist Anthony] Trollope, "solid and substantial, . . . and just as real as if some giant had hewn a great lump out of the earth." Even in his own writings, as he pointed out, the style is public. There is "none of the abstruseness of idea, or obscurity of expression, which mark the written communications of a solitary mind with itself. . . . It is, in fact, the style of a man of society." Yet this devotee of Trollope began his literary career by a ten years' retreat, and his books are precisely the expression of the solitary and the mental. Or, rather, they might be considered the resultant of the two quite opposite forces within Hawthorne; they establish "a neutral territory, somewhere between the real world and fairy-land, where the Actual and the Imaginary may meet, and each imbue itself with the nature of the other." Unable to feel any confidence in the reality of the subjective, and unable, despite the long effort of his notebooks, to come to grips with the solid earth, Hawthorne evolved his conception of the "romance." Whereas the novelist was limited to "the probable and ordinary course of man's experience," the romancer tried to create a realm

Excerpted from *Symbolism and American Literature* by Charles Feidelson Jr. Chicago: University of Chicago Press, 1953; ©1953 by The University of Chicago. Reprinted with permission.

midway between private thought and the objective world. This doctrine, which is the burden of the prefaces to *The House of the Seven Gables*, *The Blithedale Romance*, and *The Marble Faun*, betrayed an intellectual as well as a literary problem. Hawthorne was anxious not merely to draw the literary distinction between the novel and the romance, and to enter apologies for the latter, but also, and more fundamentally, to fix the status of the romance in an almost metaphysical sense. While he was granting or even insisting that "reality" belonged to Trollope, he was trying, in effect, to say what kind of reality his own work had. For the fact is that what seems at first a wholly personal problem, resulting from Hawthorne's peculiar temperament, turns out to be a reflection of the problem of the times. The Actual and the Imaginary can meet only in a theory or habit of perception. Hawthorne's comment on *Twice-Told Tales* is true of all his books: they were "attempts, and very imperfectly successful ones, to open an intercourse with the world."

CONFLICTING LITERARY METHODS

The imperfect success may be attributed at least partially to the way he put the question. Hawthorne, who was contemptuous of abstract speculation, was caught willy-nilly in a speculative dilemma, and his approach to it was oversimplified. He believed that he had only to discover suitable materials: he chose Brook Farm as the subject of *The Blithedale Romance* because that social experiment in itself had been "essentially a day-dream, and yet a fact, . . . thus offering an available foothold between fiction and reality." But the problem before him actually involved the relationship of the imagination to *any* fact, and it could be solved only by a fundamental adjustment of the mind and things, not by seeking out ready-made solutions. It was inevitable that Hawthorne should find, as he complained in preface after preface, that materials with the proper "atmosphere" were hard to come by. This faulty conception of his problem was complicated by his prejudice in favor of the physical and the rational, a bias which, if followed through, would have made any valid union of the Actual and the Imaginary not only impossible but undesirable. While he stated clearly enough that he sought to mediate between the private vision and the common-sense objective world, he was likely at the same time, adopting an apologetic tone, to speak of his work as "fancy-pictures" and "castles in the air," as though his aim were simply the amusement of cutting himself loose from any reality.

The natural outcome of this theoretical indecisiveness was Hawthorne's allegorical method; by this means, consciously or not, he evaded the issue with which he was confronted. For it is in the nature of allegory, as opposed to symbolism, to beg the question of absolute reality. The allegorist avails himself of a formal correspondence between "ideas" and "things," both of which he assumes as given; he need not inquire whether either sphere is "real" or whether, in the final analysis, reality consists in their interaction. Hawthorne's initial notes for his tales are for the most part abstract formulas, equally remote from the subjective and the objective world: "Personify the Century—talk of its present middle-age—of its youth, and its adventures—of its prospects." Such schemata point to a parallelism between the two worlds, but hardly would lead to richness either of imagination or of physical substance, and certainly would never produce a meeting in which each might "imbue itself with the nature of the other." If Hawthorne's writings tend to be thin in both respects, it is because he never fully faced the problem of knowledge which his own situation raised.

Yet his underlying purpose was always "to open an intercourse with the world," and out of this purpose arose not allegory but symbolism. The "Custom House" essay, introductory to *The Scarlet Letter*, is a portrait of the artist as symbolist in spite of himself. . . . The author's *donnée* [basic principles underlying literary work], as James would call it, is neither Imagination nor Actuality per se but a symbol whose inherent meaning is *The Scarlet Letter.* The world that the writer seeks is generated by contemplation of the symbol, not by the external yoking-together of two realms which by definition are different in kind. This integral act of perception effectually "opens" an imaginative reality. That it is not the material reality of nineteenth-century Salem becomes wholly irrelevant, since the meaning of the symbol, accreted [made larger or greater] by generations who have lived with it and in it, is continuous in time. . . .

PROBLEMS WITH HAWTHORNE'S SYMBOLS

With respect to symbolism, as in every other way, *The Scarlet Letter* is a special case among Hawthorne's works. Here, since the very focus of the book is a written sign, he has no difficulty in securing a symbolistic status for his material. The symbolistic method is inherent in the subject, just as the subject of symbolism is inherent in the method. This is only partially true of the other romances. In *The House of the Seven Gables,* *The Blithedale Romance,* and *The Marble Faun,* Hawthorne's effort to establish a symbolistic standpoint has an air of contrivance; he falls back on *ad hoc* devices. Donatello in *The Marble Faun,* for example, is associated with the Faun of Praxiteles [Greek sculptor of fourth century B.C.], and he is apprehended by Miriam, Hilda, and Kenyon in much the same way as they perceive a work of art. The imputed identity of the man and the statue serves to abstract Donatello from any objective existence and, without relegating him to the realm of sheer fancy, to locate him in the middle ground that Hawthorne wanted. Similarly, the "sylvan dance" of Miriam and Donatello is treated as "the realization of one of those bas-reliefs [low-relief sculpture] where a dance of nymphs, satyrs, or bacchanals is twined around the circle of an antique vase." Although Hawthorne's judgments on statuary and painting are crude and often amount to no more than sheer padding, the constant allusion to these arts in *The Marble Faun* has an overall function. Hawthorne is trying to suggest a situation in which everything perceived has the symbolic status of an aesthetic object. "The Bronze Pontiff's Benediction," conferred on the three friends in the market place at Perugia [a city in central Italy], is typical of a mode of perception that recurs throughout the book. The statue of the Pope seems "endowed with spiritual life" because all things can become significant in the "unexpected glimpse" which removes them from the customary world:

> There is a singular effect oftentimes when, out of the midst of engrossing thought and deep absorption, we suddenly look up, and catch a glimpse of external objects. We seem at such moments to look farther and deeper into them, than by any premeditated observation; it is as if they met our eyes alive, and with all their hidden meaning on the surface, but grew again inanimate and inscrutable the instant that they became aware of our glances.

In *The Blithedale Romance* Hawthorne makes use of another expedient. Miles Coverdale, the ill-natured aesthete [someone excessively concerned about art and beauty] who serves as narrator, views the entire action as a kind of play enacted before him. For him, the three leading figures—Hollingsworth, Zenobia, and Priscilla—form a "knot of characters, whom a real intricacy of events, greatly assisted by my method of insulating them from other relations, . . . kept . . . upon my mental stage, as actors in a drama." Again Hawthorne's purpose is to place the story in terms of aesthetic perception. But neither the imagination of Coverdale nor the artistic analogy of *The Marble Faun* can actually carry that weight, since neither is maintained fully and consistently enough. In both cases the net effect is one of coy excuse; Hawthorne is not sure of his own stand. Perhaps his books are to claim an aesthetic reality; perhaps they merely constitute an "unreal" opposite of the physical world; perhaps they must take refuge in a noncommittal parallelism between Imagination and Actuality. He himself was well aware of one aspect of this indecision—the split within him between the man of "fancy" and the admirer of Trollope. He did not see so clearly that this opposition was transected by another, more debilitating conflict—between the symbolist and the allegorist.

THE ALLEGORY-SYMBOL PROBLEM UNSOLVED

The truth is that symbolism at once fascinated and horrified him. While it spoke to his "sensibilities," it evaded "the analysis of [his] mind." On the one hand, the symbol was valuable precisely because it transcended analytic thought; on the other hand, that very transcendence, with its suggestion of the unconventional, the novel, the disorderly, was potentially dangerous. The letter had "deep meaning," but the letter was scarlet, and Pearl, its embodiment, had no "principle of being" save "the freedom of a broken law." Hawthorne dwells on the elusiveness, the rationally indefinable quality of Pearl, who "could not be made amenable to rules, . . . whose elements were perhaps beautiful and brilliant, but all in disorder; or with an order peculiar to themselves, amidst which the point of variety and arrangement was difficult or impossible to be discovered." Allegory was the brake that Hawthorne applied to his sensibility. For allegory *was* analytic: allegory was safe because it preserved the conventional distinction between thought and things and because it depended on a conventional order whose point of arrangement was easily defined. The symbolistic and the allegorical patterns in Hawthorne's books reach quite different conclusions; or, rather, the symbolism leads to an inconclusive luxuriance of meaning, while allegory imposes the pat moral and the simplified character. This predicament comes to the surface in an absurd conversation between Kenyon and Miriam toward the end of *The Marble Faun.* Since Donatello has been symbolically identified with the statue of the Faun, in which "the characteristics of the brute creation meet and combine with those of humanity," his crime, from this point of view, is a necessary step in his attainment of fully human qualities. At the same time, Donatello has been associated with Adam, and his crime with the Fall of Man. The combination of these two meanings in the one character forces a reinterpretation of orthodox Evil. "Was the crime," Miriam asks, "in which he and I were wedded—was it a blessing, in that strange disguise?" This is more than Kenyon can stomach: "You stir up deep and perilous matter, Miriam. . . . I dare not follow you into the unfathomable abysses whither you are tending. . . . It is too dangerous." And Hawthorne himself repudiates "these meditations, which the sculptor rightly felt to be so perilous." He falls back on the simple morality of Hilda, a purely allegorical creature equipped with white robe, tower, lamp, and doves.

Yet there can be no doubt that Hawthorne experienced the attraction of inverted values—the extreme form of that anti-conventional impulse which is inherent in symbolism. In the Roman Eden, he ventures to say, "the final charm is bestowed by the malaria. . . . For if you come hither in summer, and stray through these glades in the golden sunset, fever walks arm in arm with you, and death awaits you at the end of the dim vista." The "piercing, thrilling, delicious kind of regret" which these thoughts arouse in him points in an obvious direction: "Aux objets répugnants nous trouvons des appas [we find attraction in repugnant things]." [French writer Charles Pierre] Baudelaire stood at the end of the dim vista. If Hawthorne was unduly anxious about the freedom of symbolic meaning, it may be to his credit that he had some inkling of how far that method could go.

The Development of Hawthorne's Romanticism

Morse Peckham

Morse Peckham analyzes the way Nathaniel Hawthorne's romantic characters and themes develop. Like other romantic writers, Hawthorne wrote about guilt, alienation, and the past. In Hawthorne's works, a guilty character develops self-identity while alienated from society. The character accepts alienation, exploits society's guilt, and finds a moral connection based on empathy with others. When the character is ready to reenter society, he or she is also ready for redemption. Peckham argues that Hawthorne handled most of these romantic problems easily, but that he never mastered the theme of social redemption, wherein the romantic individual transforms society.

Coming to Hawthorne once again after an interval of twenty years, I was struck by two features. First is the extraordinary quality of Hawthorne at his best. Even *Fanshawe* showed at once that here was a man of astounding literary gifts, and *The Scarlet Letter* is the only novel to which I would ascribe the word "perfect." The second thing was that I encountered no themes with which European Romanticism had not made me familiar. This does not mean that Hawthorne was a mere imitator, or that his version of Romanticism was not unique. But that uniqueness does not make him peculiarly American. The great European Romantics were as different from each other as he was different from them. Each major author—and almost every minor one—discovers, examines, and proposes solutions to the Romantic problems in his own manner.

In his early short stories and sketches Hawthorne was particularly concerned with three Romantic themes: guilt, alien-

Excerpted from *The Triumph of Romanticism* by Morse Peckham; ©1970, University of South Carolina Press. Reprinted by permission of the University of South Carolina Press.

ation, and historicism [the theory that conditions of history determine events, putting them beyond human control]. These three are so intimately intertwined in his work, as in most Romantics, that it is extremely difficult to separate them. In terms of cultural development, Hawthorne, with [British Romantic poet Lord] Byron, is the great exponent of Negative Romanticism, and his efforts to understand the nature of guilt and to devise a strategy to be free from it while preserving its advantages is a central Romantic problem. It can be done only—or at least has been done only—by postulating a self independent from social role. Once this has been done, the guilt can then be seen as a strategy for achieving the self; and alienation can be interpreted not as the punishment for guilt but as the opportunity for achieving an independent self, one which can morally transcend the society and the culture. Guilt and alienation, therefore, are something to be exploited, and one of the most important techniques for that exploitation is historicism. . . .

The Romantic historicist used the past for a double, interconnected purpose. On the one hand it was a means for separating oneself from society. As such it has often been criticized as emotionally regressive, as mere nostalgia, and perhaps it would be were it not for the use the Romantic made of that historical separation or alienation. In any institution the individual who knows its history has an instrument for analysis and a means of defense against mindless surrender to its current values. He can be aware of the failure of the institution to fulfill its avowed intentions and its social function. So we find in Hawthorne two kinds of guilt, that of the individual and that of New England society. His first notable exploration of the latter is to be found in "My Kinsman, Major Molineux." The strategy of the alienated by which he relieves his own guilt of alienation by locating guilt in the society is by now a relatively standardized device, but at the time of Hawthorne it was reasonably innovative, particularly in this country. It is a self-justifying strategy in a special sense, for it postulates and confirms the self in opposition to the social role. Romantic historicism, therefore, is never an end in itself but a strategy for placing the current social conditions in an ironic perspective, and Hawthorne's historicism, though it has its particular character, is a standard Romantic variety.

THE THEMES OF SELF-REDEMPTION AND EMPATHY

Once the self has been redeemed from society it can be explored in its own terms, and for this purpose Hawthorne developed his peculiar use of emblematic [symbolic] allegory, which reaches its perfection in *The Scarlet Letter*. This technique, though Hawthorne's is different from that of European writers, creates analogies between self and not-self, between personality and the world. . . . Henceforth Hawthorne's theme is the redemption of the self through the acceptance and exploitation of what society terms the guilt of the individual but which to the Romantic is society's guilt. The two themes can be seen in their relation to one another if one juxtaposes the virtually contemporaneous "The Maypole of Merry Mount" and "The Minister's Black Veil." Nevertheless, the Romantic self cannot be established until it has found a relationship with others, and the normal Romantic relationship of this sort is empathy. The self has no real existence unless it affirms the existence of other selves, and that affirmation is the basis of Romantic morality. . . .

AMERICAN ROMANTICISM

Romanticism in America was a transplanted version of romanticism in England and Europe. In America, Ralph Waldo Emerson and Henry David Thoreau articulated romantic ideas in their transcendentalism. Rod W. Horton and Herbert W. Edwards explain the difference between European and American romanticism in Background of American Literary Thought.

While transcendentalism was in many ways peculiar to New England, it can perhaps be best understood as a somewhat late and localized manifestation of the European romantic movement. The triumph of feeling and intuition over reason, the exaltation of the individual over society, the impatience at any kind of restraint or bondage to custom, the new and thrilling delight in nature—all these were in some measure characteristic of the American counterpart of the movement of which [poet William] Wordsworth and [poet Samuel Taylor] Coleridge were the center in England and which inspired German idealist philosophy in Europe. In New England, however, romanticism assumed a predominantly moral and philosophical tone, the former having its foundations in the persistence of Puritan idealism, the latter springing largely from the writings and personality of [Ralph Waldo] Emerson.

Rod W. Horton and Herbert W. Edwards, *Background of American Literary Thought.* New York: Appleton-Century-Crofts, 1952.

Whether Hawthorne arrived at the perception of empathy by himself or derived it from earlier Romantics is irrelevant.

Certainly, it is one of the central themes of *The Scarlet Letter.*
Chillingworth is evil because he used, in his comfortless old
age, Hester as an object. Thereafter—one of Hawthorne's most
subtle points—he is emotionally dependent upon the woman
whose self he has violated. Dimmesdale also has violated both
Hester and himself by his failure to acknowledge publicly his
guilt and his love. Pearl, however, who has grown up in anti-
social innocence and is therefore not human, becomes human
and eventually, we are assured, a splendid woman by her sudden experience of empathy for her dying father. Hester, in
proper Romantic fashion, accepts her guilt, locates the source
of that guilt in society, embroiders her *A* with great splendor,
and becomes a free and self-substantiating self, transcending
the moral limitations of her world.

THE ROMANTIC SELF RE-ENTERING AND REDEEMING SOCIETY

But at the end of the book, in her return to her hut, Hawthorne
touches, rather gingerly, the next stage of Romantic development, Transcendentalism, the attempt of the free Romantic
self to re-enter society and to redeem it. That problem was to
baffle him for the rest of his life.

In *The House of the Seven Gables*, one of the most magical
and exquisitely accomplished works in European fiction [Haw-
thorne wrote like European Romantic writers], he attempts to
deal with the problem with the utmost delicacy. But perhaps
that word does him a little too much credit. Perhaps the apparent delicacy is really a gingerliness, as if he were a little afraid
to engage too seriously with the theme of social redemption.
The house itself and its inhabitants have certain resemblances
to [British poet Alfred Lord] Tennyson's "Lady of Shalott" and
"Marianna," which are both, particularly the latter, very
Hawthornesque works, with something of Hawthorne's odd
use of emblems. In the "Lady of Shalott" Tennyson is directly
engaged with the relation of alienated Romantic to society, of
tower to city. And the house is such a tower. We even have in
Holgrave the wandering Transcendentalist artist who redeems
the past, the guilt of the social order, and releases the impris-
oned, although this was more than the Lady-of-Shalott-as-
artist could do. Nevertheless, if this is the theme, those who
have been freed from the past and social guilt move not from
the tower into the city, but merely into another tower, delightfully modern, to be sure, but also built by Judge Pyncheon on
a foundation of social guilt. Are we supposed to be aware of
this? I think not. Rather I suspect that Hawthorne got a little

more started than he could quite manage.

Hence, perhaps, the element of savagery in *The Blithedale Romance*, in which the theme of social redemption is directly in the foreground, and is thoroughly mauled, and yet regretfully, too. It appears that Hawthorne has so far entered into the second stage of Romanticism—*The House of the Seven Gables* having as one of its central themes decision and action—that the world is no longer seen as having an analogical value but rather as having no value at all. "More and more I feel that we had struck upon what ought to be a truth. Posterity may dig it up, and profit by it." It is typical of many Transcendentalist statements. The artist and the thinker can present models of world redemption, but that redemption can actually take place only in the future. At any rate, the possibility of world redemption is the only basis for re-entry into society, as Hawthorne indicates in his perhaps too self-consciously amusing remarks about [Hungarian revolutionary leader Lajos] Kossuth.

THE PROBLEM OF THE PAST: FREEDOM OR CONNECTION

But another theme begins to appear, a matter which now involved Hawthorne in the gravest difficulties, the theme of American simplification, that notion that was so common among American Romantic Transcendentalists; not only is world redemption possible, but America is the predestined place for it to happen. Hawthorne has now emerged sufficiently into the world to encounter directly the peculiar problem of the American artist I have already discussed, the desire for the complexity of high-level culture in an environment turned in the direction of simplification and reductionism. The problem had first appeared faintly in the personality of Holgrave, the photographer, the new man. Further, Hawthorne was by now no longer a provincial. He had been exploring the Romantic themes which had been explored in Europe in the first quarter of the century. Emerging on the European stage, he was, in the 1850's, and in Europe, out of phase. The most advanced Romantics had already gone beyond a stage he was just beginning to struggle with. But his further progress was blocked by the confusion between the absurdities of American frontierism, of *"Amerika, du hast es besser* [America, you have it better]," and Romantic Transcendental world redemption. It was not, of course, a confusion from which he alone suffered.

On the contrary, he was aware that some baffling snarl was before him. He made four attempts [at writing a novel] to understand the problem. Three of them proved abortive, and the fourth probably would have failed had he not died. It is not surprising that after his first attempt he should have carried to completion *The Marble Faun.* Here was the theme, or a theme, of *The Scarlet Letter* all over again, in a new setting and in some ways more richly developed, the humanizing power of guilt and empathy. The faun is a kind of fusion of Hester and Pearl. But at the end of the book he is in prison. There is scarcely a hint of Hester's re-entry into society from above. That is, so long as he did not attempt that Transcendentalist theme, Hawthorne could finish a novel.

His difficulty was that he could not locate his problem. The four abortive efforts, therefore, consist of four permutations of the same factors: the footstep, or the guilt of society; the spider, the guilt of the individual; the elixir of life, the self; and the inheritance. The first three he could handle easily, but the last was too much for him, for in that emblem was adumbrated [foreshadowed] two inextricably confused themes, the relation of the United States to England, of America to Europe, and the redemption of society by freeing it from the past. On the one hand he was politically too sophisticated as well as far too alienated to imagine that the self-conception of his proper fellow citizens as representations of the new Adam was anything but self-inflationary illusion. On the other hand, he was intellectually and culturally too sophisticated, too modern, to be able to enter fully into the Transcendentalist vision, which was already an outmoded stage of Romanticism, at least for the advanced. Moreover, he was apparently unwilling or unable to take the essential step in moving from Transcendentalism to Objectism [emphasis on objects in literature, rather than on feelings and thoughts], the stripping away of divine authority from the self, the naked exposure of subject to object, though, again in a gingerly fashion, he moved in that direction. When Hilda shrinks from Kenyon's daring move that way, is it Hawthorne who shrinks, or is Hawthorne deferring to his public?

One of the marks of Transcendentalism is a fantastic extravagance of style, as in [British essayist Thomas Carlyle's] *Sartor Resartus* or the music of [Hungarian composer Franz] Liszt. By setting the work in Rome, with its churches and catacombs, and in Tuscany [a region in northwest Italy], with its old castles and pagan traditions, Hawthorne achieves the equivalent of stylistic extravagance. I would suggest then that Hawthorne's difficulty with the four efforts to write the same novel lay in the fact that he could neither get to the ultimate weakness of the Transcendentalist position nor move out of it into full abandonment of soul for self because in his way was the confusion between Transcendentalism and Americanism. The heart of the problem lay in the frightful paradox of the artist and intellectual in America, which has made it so difficult for the American artist to understand himself as either American or artist, the fact that there seems to be every reason that this country should be a place of magnificent opportunity but is, as one lives in it, so terribly constricting to the kind of man who needs desperately to live at the highest cultural level. Did Hawthorne's illness deprive him of his energy to solve his problem, or did the problem and his failure to solve it make him ill? Or was his real problem his incipient movement into Objectism?

Hawthorne's Female Characters

Randall Stewart

Randall Stewart writes that Nathaniel Hawthorne created three kinds of female characters from real-life
women he knew and from characters first sketched in
his earlier works. There are wholesome New England
girls, such as Phoebe in *The House of the Seven Gables*.
Hawthorne's graceful women, such as Priscilla in *The
Blithedale Romance*, are more delicate. Finally,
Hawthorne creates rich, exotic women, such as Hester
in *The Scarlet Letter*. Hawthorne saw qualities in his
wife Sophia that he attributed to all three kinds of
female characters.

Hawthorne's heroines may be classified . . . according to three
general types: first, the wholesome New England girl, bright,
sensible, and self-reliant; second, the frail, sylph-like creature, easily swayed by a stronger personality; and, third, the
woman with an exotic richness in her nature.

THE WHOLESOME NEW ENGLAND GIRL

Whether Ellen Langton in *Fanshawe* is a description of an
actual girl whom Hawthorne knew and perhaps loved, or is
merely an imaginary portrait of his youthful ideal, it is impossible to say. But it is significant of Hawthorne's preferences in
these matters that Ellen is the prototype of several heroines in
later stories, including Phoebe in *The House of the Seven
Gables* and Hilda in *The Marble Faun*, and that in many qualities she is an anticipation of Sophia Peabody. In Ellen's dark
eyes one may read "pure and pleasant thoughts." She has "the
gayety and simple happiness, because the innocence, of a
child." After she became a member of Dr. Melmoth's somber
household, "the sunny days seemed brighter and the cloudy
ones less gloomy." She possessed both "a large fund of plain

From Randall Stewart's Introduction to *The American Notebooks* by Nathaniel Hawthorne; ©1932, Yale University Press.

sense," and an esthetic faculty which was expressed in the daily decoration of her room with wild flowers. Differing, however, from Mrs. Hawthorne, whose linguistic knowledge was considerable [she read Latin, Greek, and Hebrew and studied German], Ellen prefers reading an old romance to pursuing a course of instruction in the learned languages, proffered by Dr. Melmoth.

Susan in "The Village Uncle" (1835) [published in *Twice-Told Tales*] has an interesting place in the development of this type. She is "a frank, simple, kind-hearted, sensible, and mirthful girl," scattering sunshine upon gloomy spirits. She keeps a shop where "gingerbread men and horses, picture-books and ballads, small fish-hooks, pins, needles, sugar-plums, and brass thimbles" are offered for sale, thus antici-pating the role of Phoebe. There is reason for believing that the sketch of Susan was based upon an actual person. Haw-thorne's sister, Elizabeth, wrote Julian Hawthorne [Haw-thorne's son, who published *Hawthorne and His Wife*]:

> About the year 1833, your father, after a sojourn of two or three weeks at Swampscott, came home captivated, in his fanciful way, with a "mermaid," as he called her. He would not tell us her name, but said she was of the aristocracy of the village, the keeper of a little shop. . . . You will find her, I suspect, in "The Village Uncle." . . . He said she had a great deal of what the French call *espièglerie* [mischievousness].

The notebooks afford abundant evidence that Hawthorne continued to observe pretty girls with interest and to record his observations. In the Augusta journal, one finds lively sketches of Nancy, "a pretty, black-eyed, intelligent servant-girl" with a piquant countenance, and of the "frank, free, mirthful daugh-ter of the landlady" with whom Hawthorne carried on a flirta-tion. The quality of *espièglerie*, particularly admired in Susan, is the salient characteristic of "our table-waiter, Eliza Chase-boro," whom Hawthorne observed at North Adams.

Although such characters as Faith Brown in "Young Goodman Brown" (1835), the nameless girl in "David Swan" (1837), Faith Egerton in "The Threefold Destiny" (1838), and Eve in "The New Adam and Eve" (1843) are very lightly sketched, it is obvious that these women, like Ellen and Susan, possess cheerfulness, prettiness, and a simple-minded domes-ticity.

The character of Phoebe is of special interest because of its derivation from several prototypes. Just as Ellen Langton promptly assumes a large share of the domestic duties in Mrs.

NOTEBOOK SKETCH FOR A NEW ENGLAND GIRL

On a trip to visit his college friend Horatio Bridge in the late 1830s, Nathaniel Hawthorne observed a girl named Nancy, a servant in the home of a Captain Harriman. He describes her in his notebook as a wholesome New England girl, one of his recurring female characters.

Hints for characters—Nancy, a pretty, black-eyed intelligent servant-girl, living in Captain Harriman's family. She comes daily to make the beds in our part of the house; and exchanges a good morning with me, in a pleasant voice, and with a glance and smile—somewhat shy, because we are not well acquainted, yet capable of being made conversible. She washes once a week, and may be seen standing over her tub, with her handkerchief somewhat displaced from her white bosom because it is hot. Often, she stands with her bare arms in the water, talking with Mrs. Harriman; or looks through the window, perhaps at [Hawthorne's friend Horatio] Bridge or somebody else crossing the yard—rather thoughtfully, but soon smiling or laughing. Then goeth she for a pail of water. In the afternoon, very probably, she dresses herself in silks, looking not only pretty but lady-like, and strolls round the house, not unconscious that some gentleman may be staring at her from behind our green blinds. After supper, she walks to the village. Morning and evening, she goes a milking—and thus passes her life, cheerfully, usefully, virtuously, with hopes, doubtless, of a husband and children. Mrs. Harriman is a particularly plump, soft-fleshed, fair-complexioned, comely woman enough, with rather a simple countenance—not nearly so piquant as Nancy's. Her walk has something of the roll or waddle of a fat woman, though it were too much to call her fat. Her breasts swell out round and soft, being abundant with milk for a little she-brat of three or four months old—her first child, though she is not a very young woman. She seems to be a sociable body—probably laughter-loving. Captain Harriman himself has commanded a steam-boat, and has a certain knowledge of life.

Nathaniel Hawthorne, *The American Notebooks.* Edited by Randall Stewart. New Haven, CT: Yale University Press, 1932.

Melmoth's household [*Fanshawe*], so Phoebe "by the magnetism of innate fitness" takes Hepzibah's place in the kitchen [*The House of the Seven Gables*]. Phoebe and Ellen are alike, also, in their lack of bookishness: the educational qualifications of the former do not extend beyond those of the mistress of the village school. Phoebe also recalls Susan in certain definite respects: they are alike not only in their vocation of shop-keeping but in an engaging detail of personal appearance: both have a few freckles which are becoming rather than otherwise. Phoebe, however, owes more to Mrs. Hawthorne than to either Ellen Langton or Susan. The name itself was one which Hawthorne had used in writing to his wife. Phoebe's nose, "slightly piquant," is modeled after Sophia's, which Hawthorne refers to in a letter as "that whimsical little nose of thine." More important, Phoebe and Sophia are alike in certain spiritual qualities. Hawthorne says that his wife "is birdlike in many things." Similarly, Phoebe is "as graceful as a bird" and possesses a "natural tunefulness . . . like a bird." Hawthorne compares his wife to bright sunshine and himself to a dark cloud. Similarly, Phoebe is a "ray of sunshine" in a "dismal place." And just as Mrs. Hawthorne with happy skill transformed the Old Manse, a "musty edifice," into a "comfortable modern residence," so Phoebe by "a kind of natural magic" effected an equally remarkable transformation in the interior arrangements of the house of the seven gables. Finally, both are of a religious nature: Mrs. Hawthorne goes to church, leaving her husband at home; Phoebe, likewise, has "a church-going conscience." From these detailed comparisons, it is clear that Phoebe is a composite character whose traits are drawn partly from the fictional characters, Ellen Langton and Susan, and partly from the author's wife.

The last character in this series of wholesome New England girls is Hilda in *The Marble Faun*. She is described as "pretty at all times, in our native New England style." In her religious orthodoxy and in her moral purity, symbolized by the doves which circle about her tower, she derives from both Phoebe and Mrs. Hawthorne herself. It appears that in this heroine, however, Hawthorne incorporated even more of his wife than in the portrait of Phoebe. The latter is a blending of the lively village girl, such as Hawthorne often met on his adventurous journeys through rural New England and occasionally described in the notebooks, and Sophia in her capacity as a home maker. In *The Marble Faun*, Hawthorne has apparently forgotten those earlier feminine models of his youth and the character of Hilda becomes little more than an ideal portrait of the author's wife. This identity is particularly obvious in the account of Hilda's artistic career:

> Even in her school-days . . . she had produced sketches that were seized upon by men of taste, and hoarded as among the choicest treasures of their portfolios; scenes delicately imagined, lacking, perhaps, the reality which comes only from a

close acquaintance with life, but so softly touched with feeling
and fancy, that you seemed to be looking at humanity with
angels' eyes.

[Painter and poet] Washington Allston had encouraged Sophia
in her painting; and Hawthorne may have had in mind her
drawing of Ilbrahim, the gentle boy, in the phrase "looking at
humanity with angels' eyes." Both Hilda and Sophia succeeded better as copyists than as original painters; at times their
copies surpassed the originals. Although the crushing blow
inflicted upon Hilda by the mere knowledge of the guilt of
Miriam and Donatello finds no parallel in Sophia's life, the
experience, nevertheless, is conceived in harmony with the
almost too moral character of Mrs. Hawthorne, of whom her
sister, Elizabeth Peabody, wrote: ". . . there was one kind of
thing she could not bear, and that was, moral evil." [*Hawthorne and His Wife*].

Phoebe remains, perhaps, the most satisfactory heroine in
the group which we have just studied. With a personality more
varied and more real than Hilda's, she is closer to the New
England village life which Hawthorne had observed and
recorded in the tales and notebooks. Hilda is the product of a
later period when the author has been almost completely dera-
cinated [uprooted] from the New England soil and when his
wife has become too exclusively his pattern of pure woman-
hood.

THE SYLPH-LIKE CREATURE

To trace the lineage of Alice Pyncheon and Priscilla, one must
go back to three fragile maidens who are but slightly sketched
in the earlier tales: Sylph Etherege in the story of that name
(1838); Alice Vane in "Edward Randolph's Portrait" (1838);
and Lilias Fay in "The Lily's Quest" (1839). Sylph Etherege
was a "shy, sensitive, and fanciful" girl with a "slender and
sylph-like figure" and a nervous organization so delicate that
"every vibration of her spirit was visible in her frame." Being
too pure and spiritual for the earth, she was translated to the
spirit world and thereby escaped her diabolical antagonist.
Alice Vane is described as "a pale, ethereal creature, who,
though a native of New England, had been educated abroad,
and seemed not merely a stranger from another clime, but
almost a being from another world." Lilias Fay, like her two
precursors, was a being so delicate that "she looked as if the
summer breeze should snatch her up and waft her heaven-
ward." Her death, like that of Sylph Etherege, results not from

an external cause, but from mere inanition [exhaustion]; its true *raison d'être* [reason for existing] is the enforcement of a moral—that all joy is attended by sorrow. It may not be fantastic to suggest that the snow image in the story of that title (1850) properly belongs in this group of sylph-like maidens. Such is the ethereal grace of the image that the mother of the children supposes it to be an angel; and the gradual drooping of the snow maiden when she is brought into the warm parlor is not unlike the waning of Sylph Etherege and Lilias Fay.

Alice Pyncheon, like Alice Vane, was educated abroad. Like Sylph Etherege, she escapes her persecutor by death, which follows a wasting away of her frail form. Two new elements, however, are added to the type in the portrait of Alice Pyncheon: her sin of pride, which Hawthorne had treated before in "Lady Eleanore's Mantle" (1838); and her faculty as a medium, a role which is elaborated in *The Blithedale Romance.*

A study of the character of Priscilla affords further illustration of Hawthorne's method of mixing ingredients derived from various sources. Arriving at Blithedale in the midst of a snowstorm, Priscilla recalls to the author an earlier creation, the snow image:

> The fantasy occurred to me that she was some desolate kind of a creature, doomed to wander about in snow-storms; and that, though the ruddiness of our window-panes had tempted her into a human dwelling, she would not remain long enough to melt the icicles out of her hair.

And, again, she is described, fantastically, as "this shadowy snow-maiden, who, precisely at the stroke of midnight, shall melt away . . . in a pool of ice-cold water." If in her ethereality Priscilla recalls the snow maiden, in her physical frailty, particularly upon her arrival at Blithedale, she resembles the other heroines in this group from Sylph Etherege to Alice Pyncheon. Her kinship with the latter is especially significant in that, like Alice, Priscilla is a medium. But Priscilla's character has elements of strength as well as of weakness; and here she parts company with her precursors in Hawthorne's fiction. In describing her improving health at Blithedale and her pranks on the farm—her clambering upon a load of hay and her riding on the oxen—the author drew upon the account in the notebook of the seamstress at Brook Farm. Thus we see that Priscilla, unlike her fictional prototypes, possessed a reserve of health and normal instincts. And in the following statement of her resiliency and fortitude, the author must have had in mind Mrs. Hawthorne herself, who had succeeded, after her marriage, in partly overcoming a chronic invalidism:

> Thus, while we see that such a being responds to every breeze
> with tremulous vibration, and imagine that she must be shat-
> tered by the first rude blast, we find her retaining her equilibri-
> um amid shocks that might have overthrown many a sturdier
> frame.

To sum up, Priscilla blends qualities taken from sources
both ideal and real: her fragility, her ethereality, and her faculty as a medium were carried over from her fictional precursors; her fund of health and good humor and her tenacious
hold on life were suggested by actual persons—the seamstress
and Sophia Hawthorne.

THE WOMAN WITH EXOTIC RICHNESS

The third group of Hawthorne's women, those whose nature is
marked by a certain exotic richness, includes Beatrice in
"Rappaccini's Daughter," Hester in *The Scarlet Letter*, Zenobia
in *The Blithedale Romance*, and Miriam in *The Marble Faun*.

Beatrice [*Mosses from an Old Manse*] is a young girl,
"redundant with life, health, and energy"; her voice is "as rich
as a tropical sunset"; and her array is marked by "as much
richness of taste as the most splendid of the flowers" in her
father's garden. She is capable, on occasion, of a "queenlike
haughtiness." Hester Prynne "had in her nature a rich, voluptuous, Oriental characteristic," which is symbolized by the
elaborate embroidery on the scarlet letter. She is tall, with "a
figure of perfect elegance on a large scale." She, too, is often
haughty in her demeanor. Zenobia is a woman of "bloom,
health, and vigor" with a "spacious plan" of physical development. Her exotic beauty is symbolized by the hothouse flower
which she wears daily in her hair. Like her predecessors, she
has as much pride as a queen. Miriam's beauty, finally, is
remarkable for "a certain rich Oriental character in her face."
Although Hester and Zenobia are older and of a more ample
physical development than Beatrice and Miriam, there is, nevertheless, an obvious similarity in appearance among the four
members of this group.

These women are unique in Hawthorne's fiction, not only for
their physical appearance, but for their mental traits: they are
the only women of marked intellectual ability in Hawthorne's
stories. Beatrice's erudition was such that she was "qualified to
fill a professor's chair." Hester, in the solitude of her cottage,
enjoyed "a freedom of speculation," entertaining heterodox
thoughts which, had they been known, would have been

regarded by the community as more culpable than the sin symbolized by the scarlet letter. With the future improvement of the world, Hester was hopeful that "the whole relation between man and woman" would be established "on a surer ground of mutual happiness." Zenobia was also given to heterodox thinking: "She made no scruple of oversetting all human institutions, and scattering them as with a breeze from her fan." Like Hester, she was particularly interested in the subject of the relation between the sexes; but, unlike Hester, she was ready to take an active part "in behalf of woman's wider liberty." While it is true that Zenobia's zealous advocacy of woman's rights may have been suggested by [New England intellectual and feminist] Margaret Fuller's active interest in that subject, it is obvious, nevertheless, that this aspect of her character may be regarded as an extension and development of a similar trait in her predecessor, Hester Prynne. Miriam, likewise, is a woman of independent and subversive thought, which is contrasted with the simple, trusting orthodoxy of Hilda.

It is interesting and perhaps significant of his moral judgments that Hawthorne should ascribe sin, either explicit or suggested, to these women of exotic physical beauty and speculative mind. Hester's sin alone is explicitly stated. Is Beatrice angel or demon? The answer is not clear. The author himself did not know. But the reader suspects that Hawthorne intended that the physical poison should symbolize spiritual poison. It is vaguely hinted that in Zenobia's past life there was some culpable relationship with Westervelt [a character in *The Blithedale Romance*] which placed her in his power. Miriam's sin is concealed by the deliberate obscurity of the author's method. In one passage, however, Hawthorne assigns to Miriam conduct similar to that of Chillingworth and perhaps indicates thereby that she was under diabolical domination: ". . . fancying herself wholly unseen, the beautiful Miriam began to gesticulate extravagantly, gnashing her teeth, flinging her arms wildly abroad, stamping with her foot." Here again we see Hawthorne's method of developing his characters by drawing source material from earlier characters of his own.

Twice-Told Tales: A Blend of Stories

Roy Harvey Pearce

According to Roy Harvey Pearce, the third edition of *Twice-Told Tales* brings together stories for entertainment and stories with symbolic meaning. Nathaniel Hawthorne had written sketches and tales for gift-books, which were popular among moral, genteel ladies who liked sentimental stories. He had also written serious stories in which he explored possible meanings and invented symbols. *Twice-Told Tales* blends these two kinds of stories, which, according to Pearce, when taken together make a whole that "is surely greater than the sum of its parts."

Hawthorne's understanding of the meaning of his *Twice-Told Tales* is made quite clear in a sentence from the preface which he wrote for the third edition of 1851: "[The tales and sketches] are not the talk of a secluded man with his own mind and heart (had it been so, they could hardly have failed to be more deeply and permanently valuable), but his attempts, and very imperfectly successful ones, to open an intercourse with the world." This, in its very negativism and modesty, is a precise estimate of the genesis of the tales and sketches themselves, of Hawthorne as their author, and of the crucial place they had in his career. And it should be, if we think out its implications carefully, the twentieth-century reader's way into their meaning.

Having graduated from college in 1825, Hawthorne moved to his mother's home in Salem and set out, simply enough, to make himself into an author. The years he spent there are those which have come to be called "lonely." They were lonely, however, not because of any sad, frustrated withdrawal from day-to-day busyness, but because Hawthorne determined to work hard at his new-found vocation. Bitterly ashamed of the miseries of his first novel, *Fanshawe* (pub-

From Roy Harvey Pearce's Introduction to *Twice-Told Tales* by Nathaniel Hawthorne; ©1954 by Roy Harvey Pearce. Reprinted by permission of the author.

lished anonymously in 1828), he soon found that his own talent was for short fiction—fortunately, for this was the only market readily available to him. If he was to hold his intercourse with the world, that is to say, he had to speak in forms which the world allowed, even demanded. Magazines and giftbooks, these constituted the media in which the aspiring young American author of Hawthorne's time could get published. And the forms for those media were the tale and the sketch. True enough, Hawthorne planned more than once to write groups of tales and sketches somehow linked into a whole; but he could not get a publisher for them. When he did get a publisher in 1837, it had to be through the help of the hack-editor, Samuel Goodrich, to whose magazines and giftbooks he had for some time, under various pseudonyms [a false name], been a main contributor; and even so, the cost of publication of the first edition of *Twice-Told Tales* (about half the size of the present volume, which derives from the second edition) had to be, without Hawthorne's knowledge, guaranteed by a friend. Once the *Tales* were published, however, Hawthorne had begun to open up an intercourse with the world—and as much on his terms as the world's.

A DEVELOPING REPUTATION

He continued, now with a small reputation, to write tales and sketches, so that in 1842 it was possible for another publisher to issue a two-volume edition of the *Tales*. There was another collection, *Mosses from an Old Manse*, in 1846, and then the full flowering of genius in a novel, with *The Scarlet Letter* in 1850. These details are worth recalling here because they let us understand further Hawthorne's own evaluation of the *Twice-Told Tales* when they were reissued the following year. *The Scarlet Letter*, so publishing records show, was an unexpected success, and Hawthorne's publishers wanted to capitalize on that success quickly. So they asked him to rush them a preface for a reprinting of the second edition of the *Tales*, even told him they were in so much of a hurry that he would not have to read proof on the text proper. Thus he was faced with a curious problem. Having finally discovered himself as author, having finally done what he wanted to do without a preponderant regard for his audience, he was now faced with the necessity of reintroducing himself to his new-found readers. Those who knew him as the author of *The Scarlet Letter* would meet him as the author of a series of tales and sketches, some deadly serious, some sentimental, but all written with the exigencies [pressing needs] of publication in mind.

In his own gentle way he treated the matter ironically, asked his readers to remember his situation when he had written the tales and sketches, called attention to the fact that they had been written for a popular, gift-book audience, and emphasized that they were meant to communicate directly and simply. . . . In it Hawthorne tries to make a whole out of a series of scattered pieces. Trying to do so, he gives us an insight into his own conception of his art and lets us more clearly conceive and judge of the tales and sketches he was introducing.

What we should note, on this basis, is the relation between the uncertainty and tenuousness of the weaker work in the

SELECTING STORIES

When the third edition of Twice-Told Tales *was published, Nathaniel Hawthorne was an established writer, but he was unknown when he planned the first edition. In* Hawthorne's Early Tales, A Critical Study, *Neal Frank Doubleday explains the importance of careful selection for the first edition.*

When Hawthorne went about assembling the eighteen pieces for his volume, he selected from forty or more pieces that had been printed in magazines, in the Salem *Gazette*, and in the *Token*. Certainly he made his selection carefully. We need to remember that, although nowadays even devoted students of Hawthorne do not often consider his collections as literary entities, their make-up and proportion were doubtless important to him. Moreover, he was putting his name to his work for the first time. He was not only presenting a selection of his work: he was presenting himself as a literary person. He was for the first time fully considering his relationship with the public he hoped would support his work. These matters are not extraneous to Hawthorne's function as a literary artist. . . .

These eighteen tales and sketches had been printed during eight years; they had been written during ten or twelve; they are less than half of what Hawthorne had available.

Clearly Hawthorne had a problem in his selection. [Hawthorne's sister-in-law] Elizabeth Peabody remembered him saying that his experience before the publication of *Twice-Told Tales* was like that of "a man talking to himself in a dark place." A writer of any sort needs a response to what he has written; if he tries to assess his own work without it, he is beset by continual misgivings. Hawthorne may have had responses we do not know about, but they were few at best.

Neal Frank Doubleday, *Hawthorne's Early Tales, A Critical Study.* Durham, NC: Duke University Press, 1972.

volume (for example "Sunday at Home," "Little Annie's Ramble," and "A Rill from the Town Pump") and the sureness and strength of the stronger (for example, "Wakefield" and "The Gentle Boy"). Abstractly considered, the method of these pieces, and of the classes they represent, is pretty much the same: a seizing upon a concrete situation, an exploration of its possible meanings—an invention, that is, of a symbol. But in the former class there is not much there to begin with, merely a gentle *frisson* [a moment of intense excitement], a feeling that something must be here. While in the latter the narrative pattern is vital from the very beginning; in effect, it carries its own meaning, and Hawthorne's task is to create the form whereby that meaning will strike the reader as powerfully as it seems to have struck the author.

Why, we may ask, this apparent lack of power to discriminate between the genuine and the seeming-genuine, between the truly found and the apparent? There was, of course, the necessity to write, as if for a living. And in the gift-books one wrote predominantly for genteel, sentimental, highly moral ladies. But beyond that: there was the unity of Hawthorne's temperament, of his mode of holding intercourse with the world, which made him (intellectual heir of seventeenth-century New England Puritanism that he was) always see, or try to see, the world as a structure of symbols—each symbol powerfully and luminously manifesting its own meaning for the artist to record, develop, and communicate. When the meaning was not there and Hawthorne wanted it to be there, he had to allegorize. His Preface to the *Tales* shows that he was dissatisfied with such allegorizing; but we should remember that he continued all his life to allegorize. Most important, we should remember that he continued to do so even as he wrote, in some of his later long fictions, work which is in the fully realized symbolic pattern of "Wakefield" and "The Gentle Boy." As a tired old man, trying to work out the novel of which "The Dolliver Romance" is the principal fragment, he noted down the governing rule of his artistic method and his temperament: "There is need of some great central event." The events of which he chose to write, from the *Twice-Told Tales* years onward, were not always sufficiently great or sufficiently central. The result was like "Sunday at Home" and the others. The important point is that Hawthorne, with full realization of what they were, acknowledged these to be as much his as was the achieved work which he preferred, as we do. For good and for bad, they are integrally part of his work, a work which taken

together—as it must be if we read the *Twice-Told Tales* with loving care—is surely greater than the sum of its parts.

TALES ANTICIPATES THE SCARLET LETTER

The best of the *Twice-Told Tales* point toward *The Scarlet Letter*
and the work which followed it. There is, above all in the tales
based upon New England legend, that brooding sense of the
past—and of its hopes, promises, betrayals, responsibilities,
and burdens—which more and more came to be Hawthorne's
primary theme, and which from him through Henry James has
come to be the theme of so much contemporary American
writing. A piece so simple in structure, at first reading so harmless, as "The May-Pole of Merry Mount," for example, contains
in itself a careful portrayal of the polarities of nineteenth- as
well as of seventeenth-century life, marks out an almost regret-
ful preference for one of them, and looks to the future in the
marriage under Puritan auspices of an anti-Puritan pair. What
is the significance of the hope expressed at the end but as a
hope for Hawthorne's own time? It is, as Hawthorne writes it
down, a living hope, derived from a living past—in an American society not too much aware that it had a past. True enough,
"The May-Pole of Merry Mount" is a small thing. But reading it,
we must see it in relation to the larger things which followed.
The *Twice-Told Tales,* indeed, record the origin and growth of a
major creative spirit and the prospect and promise of his major
creations.

Hawthorne's Tales of Brevity and Effect

Edgar Allan Poe

When he was editor of *Graham's Magazine*, Edgar
Allan Poe published a review of Nathaniel
Hawthorne's *Twice-Told Tales*. Poe, who gives but brief
comment on the essays in Hawthorne's volume, carefully defines a good tale: It should have the qualities of
brevity, unity, and effect. With this definition in mind,
Poe says that Hawthorne's tales "belong to the highest
region of Art," and he cites several examples. Poe
praises Hawthorne's imagination, his style, and his
themes and calls him a genius.

Edgar Allan Poe, an American romantic writer,
wrote poetry and short stories. His stories and poems
exemplify the ideas set forth in this review and create
effects of mystery and terror.

The book [*Twice-Told Tales* by Nathaniel Hawthorne] profess-
es to be a collection of *tales*, yet is, in two respects, misnamed.
These pieces are now in their third republication, and, of
course, are thrice-told. Moreover, they are by no means all
tales, either in the ordinary or in the legitimate understanding
of the term. Many of them are pure essays; for example,
"Sights from a Steeple," "Sunday at Home," "Little Annie's
Ramble," "A Rill from the Town Pump," "The Toll-Gatherer's
Day," "The Haunted Mind," "The Sister Years," "Snow-
Flakes," "Night Sketches," and "Foot-Prints on the Sea-Shore."
We mention these matters chiefly on account of their discrep-
ancy with that marked precision and finish by which the body
of the work is distinguished.

Of the essays just named, we must be content to speak in
brief. They are each and all beautiful, without being characterized by the polish and adaptation so visible in the tales
proper. A painter would at once note their leading or predom-

From Edgar Allan Poe, "*Twice-Told Tales*, by Nathaniel Hawthorne: A Review," *Graham's Magazine*, May 1842.

inant feature, and style it *repose.* There is no attempt at effect. All is quiet, thoughtful, subdued. Yet this repose may exist simultaneously with high originality of thought; and Mr. Hawthorne has demonstrated the fact. At every turn we meet with novel combinations; yet these combinations never surpass the limits of the quiet. We are soothed as we read; and withal is a calm astonishment that ideas so apparently obvious have never occurred or been presented to us before. Herein our author differs materially from [British essayists Charles] Lamb or [Leigh] Hunt or [William] Hazlitt—who, with vivid originality of manner and expression, have less of the true novelty of thought than is generally supposed, and whose originality, at best, has an uneasy and meretricious [superficial] quaintness, replete with startling effects unfounded in nature, and inducing trains of reflection which lead to no satisfactory result. The Essays of Hawthorne have much of the character of [American writer Washington] Irving, with more of originality, and less of finish; while, compared with [the British periodical] the *Spectator,* they have a vast superiority at all points. The *Spectator,* Mr. Irving, and Mr. Hawthorne have in common that tranquil and subdued manner which we have chosen to denominate repose; but, in the case of the two former, this repose is attained rather by the absence of novel combination, or of originality, than otherwise, and consists chiefly in the calm, quiet, unostentatious expression of commonplace thoughts, in an unambitious, unadulterated Saxon [English language]. In them, by strong effort, we are made to conceive the absence of all. In the essays before us the absence of effort is too obvious to be mistaken, and a strong undercurrent of suggestion runs continuously beneath the upper stream of the tranquil thesis. In short, these effusions of Mr. Hawthorne are the product of a truly imaginative intellect, restrained, and in some measure repressed, by fastidiousness of taste, by constitutional melancholy, and by indolence.

THE IMPORTANCE OF LENGTH

But it is of his tales that we desire principally to speak. The tale proper, in our opinion, affords unquestionably the fairest field for the exercise of the loftiest talent, which can be afforded by the wide domains of mere prose. Were we bidden to say how the highest genius could be most advantageously employed for the best display of its own powers, we should answer, without hesitation—in the composition of a rhymed poem, not to exceed in length what might be perused in an hour. Within this limit alone can the highest order of true poetry exist. We need only here say, upon this topic, that, in almost all classes of composition, the unity of effect or impression is a point of the greatest importance. It is clear, moreover, that this unity cannot be thoroughly preserved in productions whose perusal cannot be completed at one sitting. We may continue the reading of a prose composition, from the very nature of prose itself, much longer than we can persevere, to any good purpose, in the perusal of a poem. This latter, if truly fulfilling the demands of the poetic sentiment, induces an exaltation of the soul which cannot be long sustained. All high excitements are necessarily transient. Thus a long poem is a paradox. And, without unity of impression, the deepest effects cannot be brought about. Epics [long narrative poems relating the deeds of a hero] were the offspring of an imperfect sense of Art, and their reign is no more. A poem *too* brief may produce a vivid, but never an intense or enduring impression. Without a certain continuity of effort—without a certain duration or repetition of purpose—the soul is never deeply moved. There must be the dropping of the water upon the rock. [French lyric poet] De Béranger has wrought brilliant things—pungent and spirit-stirring—but, like all immassive bodies, they lack *momentum*, and thus fail to satisfy the Poetic Sentiment. They sparkle and excite, but, from want of continuity, fail deeply to impress. Extreme brevity will degenerate into epigrammatism [qualities of a short, clever poem]; but the sin of extreme length is even more unpardonable. *In medio tutissimus ibis* ["You travel most safely in the middle course," from Ovid's *Metamorphoses*].

Were we called upon, however, to designate that class of composition which, next to such a poem as we have suggested, should best fulfil the demands of high genius—should offer it the most advantageous held of exertion—we should unhesitatingly speak of the prose tale, as Mr. Hawthorne has here exemplified it. We allude to the short prose narrative, requiring from a half-hour to one or two hours in its perusal. The ordinary novel is objectionable, from its length, for reasons already stated in substance. As it cannot be read at one sitting, it deprives itself, of course, of the immense force derivable from *totality*. Worldly interests intervening during the pauses of perusal, modify, annul, or counteract, in a greater or less degree, the impressions of the book. But simple cessation in reading would, of itself, be sufficient to destroy the true unity. In the brief tale, however, the author is enabled to carry out the fulness of his intention, be it what it may. During the hour of perusal the soul of the reader is at the writer's control. There are no external or extrinsic influences—resulting from weariness or interruption.

THE IMPORTANCE OF EFFECT

A skilful literary artist has constructed a tale. If wise, he has not fashioned his thoughts to accommodate his incidents; but having conceived, with deliberate care, a certain unique or single *effect* to be wrought out, he then invents such incidents— he then combines such events as may best aid him in establishing this preconceived effect. If his very initial sentence tend not to the outbringing of this effect, then he has failed in his first step. In the whole composition there should be no word written, of which the tendency, direct or indirect, is not to the one pre-established design. And by such means, with such care and skill, a picture is at length painted which leaves in the mind of him who contemplates it with a kindred art, a sense of the fullest satisfaction. The idea of the tale has been presented unblemished, because undisturbed; and this is an end unattainable by the novel. Undue brevity is just as exceptionable here as in the poem; but undue length is yet more to be avoided.

We have said that the tale has a point of superiority even over the poem. In fact, while the *rhythm* of this latter is an essential aid in the development of the poem's highest idea— the idea of the Beautiful—the artificialities of this rhythm are an inseparable bar to the development of all points of thought or expression which have their basis in *Truth*. But Truth is often, and in very great degree, the aim of the tale. Some of the finest tales are tales of ratiocination [logical reasoning]. Thus the field of this species of composition, if not in so elevated a region on the mountain of Mind, is a table-land of far vaster extent than the domain of the mere poem. Its products are never so rich, but infinitely more numerous, and more appreciable by the mass of mankind. The writer of the prose tale, in short, may bring to his theme a vast variety of modes or inflections of thought and expression—(the ratiocinative, for example, the sarcastic, or the humorous) which are not only antagonistical to the nature of the poem, but absolutely forbidden by one of its most peculiar and indispensable adjuncts; we allude, of course, to rhythm. It may be added here, *par parenthèse* [parenthetically], that the author who aims at the purely beautiful in a prose tale is laboring at a great disadvantage. For Beauty can be better treated in the poem. Not so with terror, or passion, or horror, or a multitude of such other points. And here it will be seen how full of prejudice are the usual animadversions [critical remarks] against those *tales of effect*, many fine examples of which were found in the earlier numbers of *Blackwood* [a monthly magazine published in Edinburgh, Scotland]. The impressions produced were wrought in a legitimate sphere of action, and constituted a legitimate although sometimes an exaggerated interest. They were relished by every man of genius: although there were found many men of genius who condemned them without just ground. The true critic will but demand that the design intended be accomplished, to the fullest extent, by the means most advantageously applicable.

POE AND HAWTHORNE: LITERARY PIONEERS

When Edgar Allan Poe and Nathaniel Hawthorne began writing stories, America had little serious fiction and no real literary tradition of its own. In Hawthorne: A Critical Study, *Hyatt H. Waggoner explains how Poe and Hawthorne started a literary tradition.*

In the deepest sense of the word Hawthorne was a creative writer.

He and Poe began creating an American fiction at the same time, under many of the same influences, and with results in many ways comparable. It seems to most critics today that Hawthorne had the richer imagination; yet whatever may be our judgment of the comparative merits of the two, it is clear that before them there was nothing in American fiction that either writer could take very seriously. Turning to European fiction, and especially to the Gothic tale [stories with supernaturalism and terror], each of them in his own way, but particularly Hawthorne, took what served his needs and transformed it, to create a form, a language, and a meaning that had never before existed.

Hyatt H. Waggoner, *Hawthorne: A Critical Study.* Rev. ed. Cambridge, MA: The Belknap Press of Harvard University Press, 1971.

We have very few American tales of real merit—we may say, indeed, none, with the exception of *The Tales of a Traveller* of Washington Irving, and these *Twice-Told Tales* of Mr. Hawthorne. Some of the pieces of [American writer and journalist] Mr. John Neal abound in vigor and originality; but, in general, his compositions of this class are excessively diffuse, extravagant, and indicative of an imperfect sentiment of Art. Articles at random are, now and then, met with in our periodicals which might be advantageously compared with the best effusions of the British Magazines; but, upon the whole, we are far behind our progenitors in this department of literature.

HAWTHORNE'S TALENT

Of Mr. Hawthorne's tales we should say, emphatically, that they belong to the highest region of Art—an Art subservient to genius of a very lofty order. We had supposed, with good reason for so supposing, that he had been thrust into his present position by one of the impudent *cliques* which beset our literature, and whose pretensions it is our full purpose to expose at the earliest opportunity; but we have been most agreeably mistaken. We know of few compositions which the critic can more honestly commend than these *Twice-Told Tales*. As Americans, we feel proud of the book.

Mr. Hawthorne's distinctive trait is invention, creation, imagination, originality—a trait which, in the literature of fiction, is positively worth all the rest. But the nature of the originality, so far as regards its manifestation in letters [literature], is but imperfectly understood. The inventive or original mind as frequently displays itself in novelty of *tone* as in novelty of matter. Mr. Hawthorne is original at *all* points.

It would be a matter of some difficulty to designate the best of these tales; we repeat that, without exception, they are beautiful. "Wakefield" is remarkable for the skill with which an old idea—a well-known incident—is worked up or discussed. A man of whims conceives the purpose of quitting his wife and residing *incognito*, for twenty years, in her immediate neighborhood. Something of this kind actually happened in London. The force of Mr. Hawthorne's tale lies in the analysis of the motives which must or might have impelled the husband to such folly, in the first instance, with the possible causes of his perseverance. Upon this thesis a sketch of singular power has been constructed.

"The Wedding Knell" is full of the boldest imagination—an imagination fully controlled by taste. The most captious critic could find no flaw in this production.

"The Minister's Black Veil" is a masterly composition, of which the sole defect is that to the rabble its exquisite skill will be *caviare* [reference to Shakespeare's *Hamlet*, meaning that the uneducated person will not understand]. The *obvious* meaning of this article will be found to smother its insinuated one. The *moral* put into the mouth of the dying minister will be supposed to convey the *true* import of the narrative; and that a crime of dark dye (having reference to the "young lady") has been committed, is a point which only minds congenial with that of the author will perceive.

"Mr. Higginbotham's Catastrophe" is vividly original, and managed most dexterously.

"Dr. Heidegger's Experiment" is exceedingly well imagined, and executed with surpassing ability. The artist breathes in every line of it.

"The White Old Maid" is objectionable even more than the "Minister's Black Veil," on the score of its mysticism. Even with the thoughtful and analytic, there will be much trouble in penetrating its entire import.

"The Hollow of the Three Hills" we would quote in full had we space;—not as evincing higher talent than any of the other pieces, but as affording an excellent example of the author's peculiar ability. The subject is commonplace. A witch subjects the Distant and the Past to the view of a mourner. It has been the fashion to describe, in such cases, a mirror in which the images of the absent appear; or a cloud of smoke is made to arise, and thence the figures are gradually unfolded. Mr. Hawthorne has wonderfully heightened his effect by making the ear, in place of the eye, the medium by which the fantasy is conveyed. The head of the mourner is enveloped in the cloak of the witch, and within its magic folds there arise sounds which have an all-sufficient intelligence. Throughout this article also, the artist is conspicuous—not more in positive than in negative merits. Not only is all done that should be done, but (what perhaps is an end with more difficulty attained) there is nothing done which should not be. Every word *tells*, and there is not a word which does *not* tell. . . .

In the way of objection we have scarcely a word to say of these tales. There is, perhaps, a somewhat too general or prevalent *tone*—a tone of melancholy and mysticism. The subjects are insufficiently varied. There is not so much of *versatility* evinced as we might well be warranted in expecting from the high powers of Mr. Hawthorne. But beyond these trivial exceptions we have really none to make. The style is purity itself. Force abounds. High imagination gleams from every page. Mr. Hawthorne is a man of the truest genius. We only regret that the limits of our Magazine [*Graham's Magazine*, of which Poe was editor] will not permit us to pay him that full tribute of commendation, which, under other circumstances, we should be so eager to pay.

Three Masterpieces in *Twice-Told Tales*

Neal Frank Doubleday

Neal Frank Doubleday cites three stories in Nathaniel Hawthorne's *Twice-Told Tales* that he regards as masterpieces and explains what makes them outstanding. "The Gentle Boy" portrays the deep emotional damage that results from the Puritan persecution of Quakers. In "The Minister's Black Veil," Hawthorne's ambiguity aptly conveys the mystery and loneliness of humans separated from one another. In "Dr. Heidegger's Experiment," Hawthorne skillfully uses Gothic elements to create a tension between the humorous events in the tale and their somber implications. Each story exemplifies an aspect of Hawthorne's moral concern.

"The Gentle Boy," "The Minister's Black Veil," and "Dr. Heidegger's Experiment" stand out in the *Twice-Told Tales* with special distinctness. Technically, they are very different from one another; and in them Hawthorne's moral concern seems to have three tempers. Although they are of course comparable in some respects to other Hawthorne tales, no one of them is a companion piece to any other tale. . . .

"THE GENTLE BOY"

"The Gentle Boy" has long been considered a sort of imaginative atonement on Hawthorne's part for the role the American progenitor of his family, William Hathorne, played in the persecution of the Quakers. His ancestor, Hawthorne writes in "The Custom House," "had all the Puritanic traits, both good and evil. He was likewise a bitter persecutor, as witness the Quakers, who have remembered him in their histories, and relate an incident of hard severity towards a woman of their sect, which will last longer, it is to be feared, than any record of his better deeds, although they were many.". . .

From Neal Frank Doubleday, "The Masterpieces in *Twice-Told Tales*," in *Hawthorne's Early Tales: A Critical Study*, pp. 159-64, 165-66. Durham, NC: Duke University Press, 1972. Reprinted with permission.

Yet, although most of the figures in the tale have their histor-ical analogues, they have a more than historical representative-ness, for this is the story of the hate and pride that live always in human hearts, and assume their strange disguises in the righteous and well-meaning. And it is the story, too, of the love that lives in human hearts, so often despised and rejected. . . .

The action had begun, we remember, in late October; before the winter snows are melted Ilbrahim [a Quaker boy] responds to the love the Pearsons give him, and to Dorothy's tact and understanding. Although he is over-sensitive and sub-ject to fits of depression, he is often happy in their household. But the scorn of children of his own age and their rejection beforehand of the love he would bestow upon them are most grievous to him. As spring comes on, however, Ilbrahim comes to believe that he has found one friend among the Puritan children. A boy about two years older than he is injured in a fall from a tree near the Pearson house and is cared for by the Pearsons. He is not an attractive boy, but in his suffering he appeals to Ilbrahim's necessity to love, and there seems an affection between the two.

One pleasant summer afternoon, when this lad is enough recovered to get about with a staff, Ilbrahim—who, having manifested his love for one child, no longer fears the rest—tries to join a group of children at play. The scene is at the out-set idyllic, and the men who pass by wonder why life cannot always retain this charm; "their hearts, or their imaginations" answer that "the bliss of childhood gushes from its inno-cence." The irony seems heavy-handed, but it underlines an irony inherent in experience.

When Ilbrahim joins the group, "all at once, the devil of their fathers" enters into "the unbreeched fanatics" and they attack him, displaying "an instinct of destruction far more loathsome than the bloodthirstiness of manhood." The boy Ilbrahim supposes his friend calls out encouragement to him; but when Ilbrahim struggles to "the foul-hearted little villain," he strikes Ilbrahim across the mouth with his staff. Ilbrahim thereupon gives up all effort to protect himself, and is beaten and trampled by the children. Severely injured, he is taken home by some neighbors, "who put themselves to the trouble of rescuing the poor little heretic." There is hardly a horror in nineteenth-century American literature so deep as this account of the Puritan children with the devil of their fathers in them; and certainly there is no more impressive symbol of the transmission of hate and ignorance. Ilbrahim seems to recover in body, but never in spirit, and indeed the attack of the children is the beginning of a decline. . . .

But "The Gentle Boy" has a quality beyond pathos. We recognize in the tale the ineluctable flaw in our nature, and apprehend that we can name but never fully understand human motives, that our experience, despite sages, scholars, and scientists, remains for us opaque. . . . On the night in which Ilbrahim dies, the voice of the wind comes "as if the Past were speaking." The Past speaks in this tale, as it does in other Hawthorne tales with other voices; we may again listen to this voice as attentively as we listen to others. . . .

"THE MINISTER'S BLACK VEIL"

The narrator [in "The Minister's Black Veil"] begins with an account of Mr. Hooper's congregation gathering on a Sunday morning in their various ages and conditions, for all are to be affected by the mysteries of the veil he has donned for the first time. The account of this first Sunday occupies about two-fifths of the narrative. It includes the Sunday morning service, the funeral of a young lady following the afternoon service, and an evening wedding—the rituals for what is really important in human experience. The next day Mr. Hooper's parishioners talk of little but his black veil, and their preoccupation with the veil grows so that at length it is "found expedient to send a deputation of the church, in order to deal with Mr. Hooper about the mystery." The narrator's amused remark about its result is a fine touch: the deputies pronounce the matter "too weighty to be handled, except by a council of the churches, if, indeed, it might not require a general synod."

When the deputies have failed, [Mr. Hooper's fiancée] Elizabeth endeavors to discover the secret of the veil. Her interview with Mr. Hooper is directly reported at some length. But if we are to suppose that Elizabeth has been able "to penetrate the mystery of the black veil" (and there is a suggestion that she has), we must suppose that she has not communicated her knowledge to the narrator, and he moves into summary narrative with a single sentence of transition: "From that time no attempts were made to remove Mr. Hooper's black veil, or, by a direct appeal, to discover the secret which it was supposed to hide.". . .

The narrator speaks of "an ambiguity of sin or sorrow, which enveloped the poor minister"; and when Elizabeth warns Mr. Hooper that "there may be whispers that you hide your face under the consciousness of secret sin," he answers,

"If I hide my face for sorrow, there is cause enough, and if I cover it for secret sin, what mortal might not do the same?" Even his dying speech does not preclude his having treasured up "the secret of his sin"; nor does anything the narrator says preclude it.

It is perhaps no wonder, then, that writers on the tale have tried to identify some sort of guilt or guilt feeling in the minister. Of late it has been insisted that it is a guilt Mr. Hooper—or perhaps Hawthorne himself—does not consciously recognize. The tale seems to invite such attempts, but they run into trouble.

A COUNTERIMAGE OF HAWTHORNE'S MOTHER

Critics often speculate on the extent to which an author's real-life experiences find their way into the author's fiction. Gloria C. Erlich argues that Catharine in Nathaniel Hawthorne's story "The Gentle Boy" is a counterimage, an opposite, of Hawthorne's mother and his relationship with her.

The gentle boy of this violent story is the artist as a wounded child, and his Quaker mother Catharine is a mother-figure as different from Hawthorne's own mother as is Hester Prynne [in *The Scarlet Letter*]. In both strong-willed fictional mothers Hawthorne created counterimages, negatives, of his own mother, endowing them with passion, self-direction, and personal magnetism. Bearing marked similarities as powerful females and single mothers, Hester and Catharine nevertheless differ significantly in the quality of their mothering, for Hester is mother to a daughter and Catharine to a son. Hester keeps her daughter near her and subordinates expression of her individual selfhood to maternal duty. Pearl and Hester are inseparable. In contrast, Catharine clearly values expression of her own ideas more highly than she values the maternal bond. Acting out her own needs, she permits separation from her son. . . .

If Hawthorne was indeed identifying with his child hero [in "The Gentle Boy"], he must have felt some inadmissible anger at his own mother's delegation of her parental functions to others. The emotional center of his family experience, like that of "the gentle boy," was the sundering of natural parental ties and the insufficiency of substitute ones.

Gloria C. Erlich, *Family Themes and Hawthorne's Fiction: The Tenacious Web.* New Brunswick, NJ: Rutgers University Press, 1984.

Discussion of Hawthorne's work should never proceed, it seems to me, as if his characteristic ambiguity were not ambiguity really, but a sort of puzzle set for critical acumen to solve. Hawthorne's ambiguity is one of his ways of representing his pervasive sense of mystery, a kind of humility in him. Even in a children's story, "The Minotaur," he remarks that "the heart of any ordinary man . . . is ten times as great a mystery as the labyrinth of Crete." He will not presume to solve the mystery, nor can he forget it. If one reads a Hawthorne tale recognizing the ambiguity, but accepting it as really ambiguous, he is reading the tale, it is safe to say, as Hawthorne intended it to be read, and to that extent reading it well.

This consideration applies in a special way to "The Minister's Black Veil." The narrator does not know what the veil conceals, and it conceals perhaps a "dreadful secret." A reading of the tale that disclosed the secret—could it do so—either as a sinful act or a psychological quirk would destroy the impressiveness of the symbol, destroy the very quality for which the tale exists. From time to time a "faint, sad smile" glimmers or flickers on Mr. Hooper's lips, but always in the same context, always when some one or more of his fellowmen seek an explanation of the veil. It is as if he smiles in the realization that what the questioners seek to know is at once simpler and far more complex than they can think. That faint smile lingers yet.

The central concern of the tale, indeed, is not the minister but the effect of the black veil on all of Milford. The narrator records its effect on the minister, on his ministry, on his fiancée, on the deputation of the church, on the officials who listen to his election day sermon, on the citizens of Milford, down to the "imitative little imp" who covers his face and is, as the narrator thinks the minister may be, "affrighted by himself." By the effect of the veil, Mr. Hooper becomes "a man of awful power over souls that were in agony for sin." Dying sinners shudder at the veil, but will not yield their breath without its wearer. The gloom of the veil enables him "to sympathize with all dark affections." And the veil has its effect not because Mr. Hooper's fellows do not recognize its meaning as a symbol, but because they do recognize it. "What," the minister asks at last, "but the mystery which it obscurely typifies, has made this piece of crape so awful?"

The citizens of Milford recognize, as everyone at least in some of his experience recognizes, how far alone each man and woman is. They do not put their recognition into words; few of us have been able to say what all mankind know. Sometimes a poet has said it for us; [British poet] Matthew Arnold in "To Marguerite" has. And in a poem by Hawthorne's contemporary, Christopher Pearse Cranch, there seems almost an echo of Hawthorne's tale:

> We are spirits clad in veils;
>   Man by man was never seen;
> All our deep communing fails
>   To remove the shadowy screen.
>
> Heart to heart was never known;
>   Mind with mind did never meet;
> We are columns left alone
>   Of a temple once complete.

Of this human burden Mr. Hooper has vowed to make himself, and does make himself, the "type and symbol." "The Minister's Black Veil" is a parable just in its representation of that burden.

If the tale is read as a parable, it touches us nearly. "Always the struggle of the human soul," [American writer] Don Marquis once wrote, "is to break through the barriers of silence and distance into companionship. Friendship, lust, love, art, religion—we rush into them pleading, fighting, clamoring for the touch of spirit laid against our spirit." If the tale is read as a parable, some passages become, not indications of a morbid condition in Mr. Hooper, but allegorical representations of human need. "It is but a mortal veil—it is not for eternity!" the minister says to Elizabeth. "O! you know not how lonely I am, and how frightened, to be alone behind my black veil.". . .

"Dr. Heidegger's Experiment"

The action [in "Dr. Heidegger's Experiment"] is a simple one. It begins on a summer's afternoon and ends at sunset. Old Dr. Heidegger invites four friends of his to experiment with an elixir from the Fountain of Youth. The friends are Mr. Medbourne, once "a prosperous merchant . . . now little better than a mendicant"; Colonel Killigrew, who "had wasted his best years . . . in the pursuit of sinful pleasures"; Mr. Gascoigne, "a ruined politician"; and the Widow Wycherly, who had been "a great beauty in her day," and with whom the three men had all been in love. The elixir effects a temporary restoration of their youthful spirits, if not perhaps of their youthful persons. But the influence of the elixir lasts but an hour or so. During that time Dr. Heidegger's four friends are, in their desires, attitudes, and propensities, exactly what they had been in their prime.

At the end of the tale, therefore, the doctor says that if the Fountain of Youth gushed at his doorstep, "I would not stoop to bathe my lips in it—no, though its delirium were for years instead of moments. Such is the lesson ye have taught me!" If that be the "lesson" of the tale, the implications are of greater importance. And they are the more disturbing because they arise from a comic action.

Dr. Heidegger's lesson is only the confirmation of his expectation by his experiment. His four friends learn nothing from the experiment, as they have learned nothing from their experience. They are, it is true, amused at the doctor's warning before they drink the elixir, for it is ridiculous to suppose that, "knowing how closely repentance treads behind the steps of error, they should ever go astray again." But their repentance—as so often in the rest of us—has not been contrition, only unhappiness. They take the same road they took so long before; their destiny seems the result of their own natures, their misdirection inevitable. Moreover, although each of the men has misdirected his life after his own fashion, they are equally prey to the calculating sexuality of the widow, who neither grants nor withholds her favors. It is their struggle over her that spills the remainder of the elixir, and destroys even their illusion of happiness. Dr. Heidegger, it is twice suggested, seems an embodiment of Time, "whose power had never been disputed, save by this fortunate company." But his four friends, in their illusion, feel "like new-created beings in a new-created universe," as we have lately and often been told was the characteristic American feeling. . . .

"Dr. Heidegger's Experiment" is (as it seems to me) a little masterpiece, without fault of taste or failure in tone. And it is pleasant to find that, at least this time, one of Hawthorne's editors recognized the essential excellence of a tale. In a congratulatory letter to Hawthorne about "Dr. Heidegger's Experiment," Lewis Gaylor Clark, the editor of the *Knickerbocker Magazine* wrote: I have rarely read anything which delighted me more. The style is excellent, and the *keeping* of the whole excellent."

Hawthorne probably would have thought of the tale as an allegory, but it does not have "the pale tint of flowers that blossomed in too retired a shade." The figures in the tale, although they are types, are lively ones. The vigorous tableau in which they take their parts is but an allegorical condensation of their lives, for their hearts have always been given to what cannot endure. The more or less nefarious bents of the widow's lovers emerge clearly; the widow looms in our imaginations in her "buxom prime." Dr. Heidegger's special powers and knowledge are established so disarmingly that we accept both them and the efficacy of his elixir. Although the mirror reflects only "withered grandsires ridiculously contending for . . . a shrivelled grandam," their illusion is, as we read, ours. We do not—willingly or unwillingly—suspend our disbelief: we have none to suspend.

Perhaps the special effect of the tale depends most of all on the restrained playfulness of its use of the Gothic [a style of fiction emphasizing the grotesque and mysterious]. Without the Gothic tradition, the assumptions of the tale would have been imaginatively unconvincing; with the Gothic elements used in the ordinary Gothic fashion, the tale could only have been commonplace. And the balance is yet more delicate. Hawthorne achieves a tension between the comic surface and the somber implications of the tale, so that this least pretentious tale may disturb us more than either his "blackness" or his exhortation elsewhere. In no work is his control more sure.

The House of the Seven Gables Captures the Atmosphere of Old Salem

Van Wyck Brooks

Van Wyck Brooks describes the buildings and their dark rooms, the eerie shadows, and the eccentric characters that create the atmosphere of Salem, Massachusetts, the setting of *The House of the Seven Gables*. Brooks explains how Hawthorne acquired his intimate knowledge of the seaport town. Every evening, Hawthorne took long walks during which he studied the town and its surroundings with the eye of a painter. Hawthorne, Brooks says, spent hours in old inns listening to tales and legends told and retold. These experiences transform themselves into the mood of the book, which has a dreamlike quality that moves "in a soft September light."

Hawthorne was forty-six years old when, in 1850, he wrote *The House of the Seven Gables*. He was living in a cottage in the Berkshires [in western Massachusetts], free at last after the leaden years he had spent at the Salem custom-house and famous with the fame of *The Scarlet Letter*. At forty-two, he had returned to Salem and seen the town of his birth in a kind of perspective that had haunted him ever since. At first he had felt benumbed and befogged. He had gone about his work on the ships and wharves with the dogged and silent practicality that always characterized his mundane life. But under this mask of insensibility, the poet had been brooding all the time. His bones were astir, even to the marrow. Salem, the ancient seaport of his boyhood, never loved by him, shunned indeed, loved less than ever now, and yet his own, so deeply, pressed

Van Wyck Brooks, Introduction to *The House of the Seven Gables* by Nathaniel Hawthorne. New York: Heritage Press, 1954.

against and flooded his consciousness. The flood had waited for the dam to break, for the moment of leisure and freedom when he could seat himself at his writing-desk, the desk with the secret drawers and the painted panels, which he had covered with little impish faces, as if to suggest that his world was very simple. The dam had burst with *The Scarlet Letter*, the scene of which might have been Puritan Salem. The overflow was *The House of the Seven Gables.*

OLD SALEM IN THE 1840S

The book was Salem itself, as Hawthorne saw it in these eighteen-forties. Since his boyhood there, the town had lapsed into quietude and decay; for the great days of the port, as of so many of the New England seaports, had scarcely survived the War of 1812. Only now and then, on the waterside streets, once thronged with tokens of the sea, some straggling sailor passed, "all right" for shore, with well-varnished hat and flowing ribbon and a bundle under his arms from the cannibal isles, or from India or China. Beside the dilapidated wharves the fat weeds grew; the grass choked the chinks of the cobblestones over which the drays had clattered in times past. But Salem was old in spirit, aside from its faded grandeurs. The past that hovered there had much in common with the past of the ancient ports of northern Europe where the tides of modern trade have not dispelled the Gothic fancies of the Middle Ages. Salem was still Gothic [a style suggesting the grotesque, mysterious, and desolate] in its frame of mind, here and there, at least. In its rusty, moss-grown, gabled houses still dwelt the remnants of a race that savoured of the emblems in the graveyards, the death's-heads and scythes and hour-glasses. In the mansions of Chestnut Street and Federal Street one found abundant signs of a livelier culture, together with the Oriental spoils brought home by the navigators and the merchants; but over the quiet lanes and leafy side-streets brooded the hush of earlier generations. Queer old maids with turbaned heads peered from behind the curtains; queer old simple-minded men hobbled along under the sweeping elms, "pixilated" [eccentric] creatures, many of them—a word they used at Marblehead [a town northeast of Boston]—bewildered by the fairies, half dead and buried in their houses, or buried in the morbid family pride that flourishes where life runs low.

This was the Salem which, in its bolder outlines, Hawthorne caught in *The House of the Seven Gables.* One scarcely had to invent stories there. One heard them from the inn-keepers and

HAWTHORNE'S DISCLAIMER

In the preface to The House of the Seven Gables, *Nathaniel Hawthorne explains that the house, street, and city in which his book is set had their source in his imagination. He asks his readers to consider the book a romance, not a historical record of any people or any place.*

The reader may perhaps choose to assign an actual locality to the imaginary events of this narrative. If permitted by the historical connection,—which, though slight, was essential to his plan,—the author would very willingly have avoided anything of this nature. Not to speak of other objections, it exposes the romance to an inflexible and exceedingly dangerous species of criticism, by bringing his fancy-pictures almost into positive contact with the realities of the moment. It has been no part of his object, however, to describe local manners, nor in any way to meddle with the characteristics of a community for whom he cherishes a proper respect and a natural regard. He trusts not to be considered as unpardonably offending, by laying out a street that infringes upon nobody's private rights, and appropriating a lot of land which had no visible owner, and building a house, of materials long in use for constructing castles in the air. The personages of the tale—though they give themselves out to be of ancient stability and considerable prominence—are really of the author's own making, or, at all events, of his own mixing; their virtues can shed no luster, nor their defects redound, in the remotest degree, to the discredit of the venerable town of which they profess to be inhabitants. He would be glad, therefore, if—especially in the quarter to which he alludes—the book may be read strictly as a Romance, having a great deal more to do with the clouds overhead than with any portion of the actual soil of the County of Essex.

Nathaniel Hawthorne, *The House of the Seven Gables.* New York: The Heritage Press, 1955.

sailors, from the good-for-nothings on the water-front. Ancient women, crouching by their fires, taking a turn at the spit, told the children stories. Salem, like the whole New England seacoast, bristled with old wives' tales and old men's legends; for in these quiet towns where nothing happens—except an occasional murder—history lies in transparent depths under the unstirred surface. Hawthorne had repeated some of these legends in the tales he called "twice told" because he had heard them first: tales of locked closets in haunted houses out of which tumbled piles of family portraits, tales of dismantled houses with secret chambers, black shadows, bloodstains, human bones, old maids in sad-coloured garments, women who lived in darkened rooms, misers who bathed in heaps of pine-tree shillings. One might scarcely have known what to believe, in this crepuscular [dim, like twilight] Salem; and Hawthorne was not the man to draw the line. His mind was a twilight mind. Sometimes he even doubted his own existence. He had lived as a ghost lives, for twelve years, under the eaves of the house in Herbert Street, only appearing for a walk at nightfall.

A WRITER WITH A PAINTER'S EYE

Hawthorne was "deep," as they say in the country, deep as a night-scene by Albert Ryder [an American who painted haunting forms and brooding seascapes lighted by moonlight]. His mind was bathed in a kind of chiaroscuro [an arrangement of light and dark elements in a picture] that seems to have been a natural trait; and yet it was a trait that he cultivated, half by instinct, half by deliberation. It was a pure delight in tone. He liked to throw a ghostly glimmer over scenes that he chose because they were ghostly. Why, he could hardly have said, any more than [Dutch painter] Rembrandt could have said it, or than Ryder could have explained his extraordinary love of varnish. He liked to study chimneys in the rain, choked with their own smoke, or a mountain with its base enveloped in mist, while the summit floated aloft, and, through the mist, a yellow field of rye. He liked to see a woman swathed, with her face, in a silvery veil; a man's face, with a patched eye, turning its profile towards him; an arm and hand extended from behind a screen; a smile that seemed to be only a part of a smile, seen through a covering hand; a sunbeam passing through a cobweb, or lying in the corner of a dusty floor. Dissolving and vanishing objects. Trees reflected in a river, reversed and strangely arrayed and as if transfigured. The effects wrought by moonlight on a wall. Moonlight in a familiar sitting-room, investing every object with an odd remoteness—one's walking-stick or a child's shoe or doll—so that, instead of seeing these objects, one seemed to remember them through a lapse of years. Hawthorne could never have said why it was that, after spending an evening in some pleasant room, lighted only by a fire of coals, he liked to return and open the door again, and close it and re-open it, peeping back into the ruddy dimness that seemed so like a dream, as if he were enacting a conscious dream.

HAWTHORNE'S KNOWLEDGE OF SALEM

This was the way he had seen Salem, through the lapse of years, opening the familiar door again, feeling as one feels at that moment of doubt when the mind is roused from sleep. The mood had grown to be second nature with him. He could not count the times, he wrote in his journal, during this later visit, when, as he raised his head towards the window, he felt that someone was passing through the gate. He could only perceive the presence with a sidelong glance, by a certain indirection; if he looked straight at the dim thing, behold, it was not there. This was the mood that his book conveyed, as if, in spite of all its air of daylight, he had never looked straight at Salem, as if he had always seen it over his shoulder. And indeed he had so seen it, in the earlier days, during his long evening walks, or from the window of the little room where he had sat in his flag-bottomed chair, writing out the stories that rose in his mind as mushrooms rise where the roots of an old tree are buried under the ground. That he knew his world no reader of his journal could be unaware. He had lived with the black old portraits, he had pondered over the annals of the town, sat for thousands of hours in the public-houses with old salts and fishermen and pilots, explored the coast from Marblehead to Boston, as he had explored the inland regions, on summer expeditions, from Maine to Crawford's Notch and Martha's Vineyard. No one had known New England as Hawthorne knew it. He might have invented Salem. But he had seen it with the "sidelong glance." He had preferred the "certain indirection." There always seemed to be a driving snow-storm on the other side of the window-glass, a cloud of dust in summer, a film, a veil. When he stood at the window on Sunday mornings, studying the church across the way, watching the sunlight stealing down the steeple, he stood behind the curtain.

Out of this mood had come his flock of tales, tales like evening moths and butterflies, light as clouds or flowers of early May, blooming in a woodland solitude. The novels rounded Hawthorne's world, a world like Prospero's island [in Shakespeare's *The Tempest*], half terrestrial, half an ethereal fabric, a new creation, if there ever was one, having its own present, past and future, a past in the Pyncheon family and the Province House, in Howe's Masquerade and Esther Dudley, a present in pedlars and daguerreotypists, in Shakers and vagabonds and white old maids, in fresh New England valleys and forest hollows, a future peopled with the puckish faces

that Hawthorne painted on his writing-desk. All very simple, it
might appear, simple as the brightly coloured leaves that mer-
rily drift over a sedgy stream—only that, too often, before one's
eyes, the stream sings its way out of the meadow and carries
its bright burden into the woods, where all grows dark and
baleful. But however one may feel the encircling darkness, it is
the flickering play of the sun and the leaves that sets the note
of *The House of the Seven Gables.* The story moves in a soft
September light, melting like a happy dream of Shakespeare.

The Past Revisits the Present in *The House of the Seven Gables*

Rita K. Gollin

Rita K. Gollin explains how ancestor Colonel Pyncheon's misdeeds and the Maules' subsequent curse live on as dark secrets in the gabled Pyncheon house. According to Gollin, Clifford, cheated by the present Judge Pyncheon, and his sister Hepzibah, who has lived in the house for thirty years, are the most severely affected by the wrongdoings of their ancestors. Young Phoebe Pyncheon and Holgrave, a Maule, escape the curse. When Judge Pyncheon dies, all of the present dwellers escape from the past.

When Hawthorne announces in the preface to *The House of the Seven Gables* that he "has provided himself with a moral;—the truth, namely, that the wrong-doing of one generation lives into the successive ones," the word "provided" exhibits self-mockery, but he proposes this truth seriously. The "legendary mist" of the distant past intermingles with memories of the recent past throughout the novel, especially in the troubled minds of the house's inhabitants. . . . Within that self [extended in time and space], the past intrudes on the present as the subconscious on the conscious.

THE HOUSE

In this sense, the novel presents the dream of the house, haunted by the guilt of its founder and the ghost of his victim. From the start, Hawthorne describes the house as if it were human: "The aspect of the venerable mansion has always affected me like a human countenance, bearing the traces not merely of outward storm and sunshine, but expressive also of the long lapse of mortal life, and accompanying vicissitudes

Excerpted from *Nathaniel Hawthorne and the Truth of Dreams* by Rita K. Gollin. Copyright © 1979 by Louisiana State University Press. Reprinted with permission.

[changes, difficulties], that have passed within.". . .

The house, itself old and haunted, permeates the minds of its aging inhabitants. Hepzibah has lived alone there for thirty years, isolated in her fantasies, "until her very brain was impregnated with the dry-rot of its timbers." She cannot get away from it even during her brief flight with Clifford. The house haunts her vision: as the train passes through "miles of varied scenery . . . there was no scene for her" but the seven-gabled house; "This one old house was everywhere! It transported its great, lumbering bulk, with more than railroad speed, and set itself phlegmatically down on whatever spot she glanced at." It seems to have a will of its own. Hepzibah is in that half-crazed state Hawthorne often described, when inner visions are so compelling that they displace perceived reality. During that same train ride, Clifford also carries within him the "rusty, crazy, creaky, dry-rotted, damp-rotted, dingy, dark, and miserable old dungeon" of a house.

The evil spirit that haunts the house is fixed in the portrait of its founder, Colonel Pyncheon, the man who had denounced Matthew Maule to get hold of his property. The old portrait is the demon of guilt within the haunted mind. Its resemblance to Judge Pyncheon, the present villain of the tale, continues the past into the present, as the Judge recapitulates the criminal greed of his ancestry. Although Hepzibah feels reverence for the portrait, she senses its spiritual ugliness; then she identifies Judge Pyncheon as "the very man." Phoebe has seen the portrait and learned its legend; then as she looks at the Judge she recalls Maule's curse that Colonel Pyncheon would drink blood. The gurgling in the Judge's throat "chimed in so oddly with her previous fancies about the Colonel and the Judge, that, for the moment, it seemed quite to mingle their identity." Like the dreamers in Hawthorne's earlier fiction who cannot face their dreams, Clifford is so disturbed by the portrait that he asks Hepzibah to curtain it [cover with a curtain]. . . .

CLIFFORD AND HEPZIBAH

The Pyncheons are described as a race of dreamers, and Clifford is the most melancholy and ineffectual of Hawthorne's long line of wasted and delicate dreamers. As the novel opens, he has just emerged from thirty years in jail, but he remains in mental and emotional bondage, victimized by a past he himself perpetuates. His mind is a prison, permeated by images of imprisonment. . . .

He spends so much time in innocent dreams that they read-

A Moral That Is Not a Moral

In his preface to The House of the Seven Gables, *Nathaniel Hawthorne provides a moral for his story. But he has no hope that his book will persuade any person to refrain from acquiring ill-gotten wealth. Instead, he hopes his work of fiction will achieve artistic truth.*

Many writers lay very great stress upon some definite moral purpose, at which they profess to aim their works. Not to be deficient in this particular, the author has provided himself with a moral;—the truth, namely, that the wrong-doing of one generation lives into the successive ones, and, divesting itself of every temporary advantage, becomes a pure and uncontrollable mischief;—and he would feel it a singular gratification, if this romance might effectually convince mankind—or, indeed, any one man—of the folly of tumbling down an avalanche of ill-gotten gold, or real estate, on the heads of an unfortunate posterity, thereby to maim and crush them, until the accumulated mass shall be scattered abroad in its original atoms. In good faith, however, he is not sufficiently imaginative to flatter himself with the slightest hope of this kind. When romances do really teach anything, or produce any effective operation, it is usually through a far more subtle process than the ostensible one. The author has considered it hardly worth his while, therefore, relentlessly to impale the story with its moral, as with an iron rod,—or, rather, as by sticking a pin through a butterfly,—thus at once depriving it of life, and causing it to stiffen in an ungainly and unnatural attitude. A high truth, indeed, fairly, finely, and skilfully wrought out, brightening at every step, and crowning the final development of a work of fiction, may add an artistic glory, but is never any truer, and seldom any more evident, at the last page than at the first.

Nathaniel Hawthorne, Preface to *The House of the Seven Gables.* New York: The Heritage Press, 1955.

ily cross the boundaries of sleep: "He sometimes told Phoebe and Hepzibah his dreams, in which he invariably played the part of a child, or a very young man." Reliving his childhood through dreams, he can even correctly remember the pattern of his mother's dress. In this delicate state of "second growth," dreams insulate him from reality like a robe "he hugged about his person, and seldom let realities pierce through; he was not often quite awake, but slept open-eyed, and perhaps fancied himself most dreaming, then." Lingering close to childhood, he enjoys "brilliant fantasies"; he went to sleep "early, as other children do, and dreamed of childhood.". . .

During the thirty years Hepzibah lived alone in the confines of the house, she bewildered herself with "fantasies of the old time. . . . She needed a walk along the noonday street, to keep her sane." David Halliburton's comment on Roderick and Madeline Usher [characters in Edgar Allan Poe's "The Fall of the House of Usher"] applies to Hepzibah and her brother: they "face a future that is also, strangely, the past, for they can only become, in a manner of speaking, what they already were. Prisoners of time, they are equally prisoners of space; in this work the hermetic space of the chamber is expanded into an entire house and its environs." But unlike Clifford, Hepzibah is sustained by a strong passion, love for her brother. For his sake she begins her venture as a shopkeeper, though her fantasies reveal how she dreads it. No "flattering dream" that her shop might help the community sustains her; her despair increases when "some malevolent spirit" unrolls a panoramic vision of magnificent stores throughout the city; and later she takes refuge in fantasies of sudden wealth. When Clifford returns home, the joy long chained "in the dungeon of her heart" uneasily finds release, and intermittently a black "spectral sorrow" replaces it. These emotions disturb her yet make her flexible enough to act as Clifford's protector.

After the Judge's death, she wanders around the house, wondering if she is dreaming. Then, during the brief interval on the train when Clifford's will is strong, she relinquishes hers, "like a person in a dream, when the will always sleeps." She feels impotently adrift in a nightmare throughout the train ride, yet that feeling is a curious safeguard: if she were certain she was awake, she might go completely mad. For a time she endures the dreamer's worst penalties: loss of will, loss of sanity, loss even of identity. Nonetheless her sense of responsibility remains intact; and when Clifford again becomes torpid, she can conduct him home. It is as if they share a single power of will, and their identities are interdependent.

PHOEBE, JUDGE PYNCHEON, AND HOLGRAVE

As a Pyncheon, Phoebe is also a dreamer, though of a far different kind. During her first night in the house, her dreams, "being such cheerful ones, had exorcised the gloom, and now haunted the chamber in its stead." She is a force of physical and emotional health, though she is sensitive to Judge Pyncheon's evil from the start. "Through the thin veil of a dream" she becomes conscious of Clifford's fragile presence, recognizing his erratic footsteps the next day as those she had heard "as through her dream." The gloomy house modifies her gay spirits in the course of the novel, but with increasing maturity she can give Clifford the warm understanding his recovery requires, and she can maintain her own health by the "moral medicines" Hawthorne frequently prescribed. She regularly leaves the confines of the house for seashore walks, lectures, and concerts, and she distracts herself by reading the Bible and thinking about her village home. She is never confused about reality, never absorbed by fantasy. Only for the moment when she drowsily listens to Holgrave's story of Alice Pyncheon is her moral balance in real danger: "A veil was beginning to be muffled about her, in which she could behold only him, and live only in his thoughts and emotions." She almost becomes, like Alice, a prototype of the impotent dreamer, with no will of her own; but Holgrave's self-control preserves her integrity.

Judge Pyncheon, the hypocritical and greedy man who had unjustly incriminated Clifford, is the incarnation of a bad dream. Hawthorne says unequivocally, "That strong and ponderous man had been Clifford's nightmare." In death he is described as a grotesque incubus, "a defunct nightmare, which had perished in the midst of its wickedness, and left its flabby corpse on the breast of the tormented one." When Hepzibah responds to his statement that Clifford knows the secret of hidden wealth in the house by saying, "You are dreaming, Cousin Jaffrey," he replies, "I do not belong to the dreaming class of men"; and we believe him. Earlier Holgrave had complained that the past lies on "the Present like a giant's dead body!" When the Judge dies, the nightmare of the Pyncheon past nears its end, and the corpse can be removed.

An extended metaphor of disgust establishes the Judge's true character, a variant of Hawthorne's recurrent metaphor for the persistence of repressed ideas. After commenting on the Judge's assumed respectability, Hawthorne makes a qualified suggestion: "Hidden from mankind—forgotten by himself, or buried so deeply under a sculptured and ornamented pile of ostentatious deeds, that his daily life could take no note of it—there may have lurked some evil and unsightly thing." He then expands this hypothesis in an elaborate image of a splendid palace with marble floors, gilded cornices, and a lofty dome. "Ah; but in some low and obscure nook—some narrow closet on the ground floor, shut, locked, and bolted, and the key flung away—or beneath the marble pavement, in a stagnant water-puddle, with the richest pattern of mosaic-work above—may lie a corpse, half-decayed, and still decaying, and diffusing its death-scent all through the palace!" He concludes the *allegoria* by equating the corpse with "man's miserable soul," then applies the indictment to Judge Pyncheon. The conceit is consistent: the Judge is a nightmare whose "unsightly" evil causes distress no matter how well it is concealed.

Holgrave is not a Pyncheon but a Maule, and Hawthorne establishes early in the novel that the Maules were believed to have "an influence over people's dreams." He is essentially an observer, though even in his daguerreotypes [early photographs] he tries to go beyond external appearances. He says to Phoebe in Melvillean [in the style of novelist Herman Melville] language, "Had I your opportunities, no scruples would prevent me from fathoming Clifford to the full depth of my plummet-line!" But he is not fair to himself: he has strong moral scruples. Hawthorne describes him as a strong and ambitious young man, though he is for a time slightly imbalanced by his obsessed involvement in the lives of the Pyncheons. Yet he finds practical outlet for that obsession by writing for magazine publication the story of Alice Pyncheon, whose ghost purportedly still haunts the house. Like Hawthorne, Holgrave is fascinated by the inner life of the house and of its occupants, past and present; and he can shape their dreamlike qualities into fiction, which in turn exerts a dreamlike effect on his audience—in his case, on Phoebe, an audience of one.

His ancestor, Matthew Maule, is the villain of Holgrave's story, a man fabled "to have a strange power of getting into people's dreams, and regulating matters there according to his own fancy, pretty much like the stage-manager of a theatre." Because the aristocratic Gervayse Pyncheon was anxious to find the valuable document hidden in the house, he allowed Matthew to mesmerize his daughter Alice. She did not find the document; but worse, when she awoke from what seemed "a momentary reverie," a power "she little dreamed of" constrained her, and her will was no longer her own. Whenever Maule demands it, her spirit must yield to his. The tale expresses Hawthorne's abhorrence of loss of will in mesmerism: Alice's abasement can only end in death. Holgrave as a Maule becomes aware that he can exert a similar power over Phoebe; but he has too much integrity, too much "reverence for another's individuality," to press his advantage. Phoebe emerges from her dreamlike trance to a beautiful moonlit evening and a new interest in Holgrave which will soon grow into love.

THE END OF THE DREAM

Rarely is the atmosphere of romance sustained by moonlight in the novel, though a dreamlike atmosphere is frequently suggested by metaphor and allusion. As Hepzibah eagerly awaits Clifford's return, Hawthorne says, "Remote and dusky, and with no sunshine on all the intervening space, was that region of the Past, whence her only guest might be expected to arrive!" One real place is equally remote and dusky, at once a preserve of the past and of romance: the house of the seven gables itself.

Hawthorne said in his preface that he wanted his tale to present the marvelous mingled with the commonplace and "to connect a by-gone time with the very Present that is flitting away from us." In his earlier fiction, dreams had established such connections. *The House of the Seven Gables* includes no full dreams and relatively few reveries; yet dream allusions weave continually on and beneath the surface of its narrative. The "legendary mist" of the past is repeatedly likened to dreams, and the mistiness is sustained through dreamlike states of mind.

The novel as a whole is thus a kind of dream narrative; and as in a dream, individual characters and even the narrator confront repressed secrets, but then return to waking reality. The bloodstained corpse in the parlor of the gloomy house at midnight can be considered their collective nightmare. And when the Judge lies dead, the long chain of Pyncheon guilt and punishment terminates. It is time for the portrait embodying the family's evil destiny to fall, and time for the hidden secrets—Holgrave's identity, the recess with its worthless treasure, and the Judge's responsibility for Clifford's imprisonment—to be revealed. The Pyncheon crimes finally avenged, the house's ghosts can rest.

In the end, the four main characters prepare to leave the house. Earlier, Holgrave had passionately declared his desire to get rid of the past. This no one can do; but he need not repeat it or live in it. In the last chapter, the "long drama of wrong and retribution is concluded," and the characters can put the house and its burdened past behind them. The communal dream is over.

The House of the Seven Gables: Hawthorne's "Second-Best Book"

Mark Van Doren

Though Nathaniel Hawthorne thought *The House of the Seven Gables* "ought to succeed better than *The Scarlet Letter*," critic Mark Van Doren calls it Hawthorne's "second-best book." In the novel, Hawthorne describes an old family mansion, its surroundings, and its inhabitants with the minute detail of a realistic painter. The descriptions make the story charming, but, Van Doren argues, Hawthorne's characters are shallow and his themes are simple. Hawthorne writes better when describing the elderly Hepzibah Pyncheon and her brother Clifford than he does in presenting Phoebe and Holgrave, Van Doren concedes, concluding that in spite of its weaknesses, the book has a haunting atmosphere and a tone that "hums."

By November 1850 Hawthorne was informing [his publisher James T.] Fields of the new romance which he would call, after some search for a title, *The House of the Seven Gables*. "I write diligently," he said, "but not so rapidly as I had hoped. I find the book requires more care and thought than *The Scarlet Letter*; also I have to wait oftener for a mood. *The Scarlet Letter* being all in one tone, I had only to get my pitch, and could then go on interminably. Many passages of this book ought to be finished with the minuteness of a Dutch picture, in order to give them their proper effect. Sometimes, when tired of it, it strikes me that the whole is an absurdity from beginning to end; but the fact is, in writing a romance, a man is always, or always ought to be, careering on the utmost verge of a precipitous absurdity, and the skill lies in coming as close as possible, without actually tumbling over. My prevailing idea is, that the book ought to succeed better than *The Scarlet Letter*, though I

Excerpted from Mark Van Doren, *Nathaniel Hawthorne* (New York: Viking, 1949); ©1949 by William Sloane Associates, Inc.

have no idea that it will." After finishing it in 1851 he wrote to [his friend Horatio] Bridge: "*The House of the Seven Gables,* in my opinion, is better than *The Scarlet Letter....* I think it a work more characteristic of my mind, and more proper and natural for me to write." The one fear he confessed to both Fields and Bridge was that the contemporary setting of the new book would seem inconsistent with its "romantic improbabilities." "I don't believe it will take like the former one. The preliminary chapter was what gave *The Scarlet Letter* its vogue." But the book did take, even better at the beginning than its predecessor. If Judge Pyncheon was a portrait of Upham [Unitarian minister who investigated witchcraft], as [Hawthorne's sister] Louisa and others assumed, this mattered little in Salem and elsewhere not at all. Nor did it matter in the long run that there had once been a Pyncheon family in Salem, whose descendants now complained that Hawthorne wronged them. Hawthorne had known nothing of these Pyncheons, nor had he expected other families to believe he was caricaturing them. So many believed it, and said so, that by June 1851 he was writing to Fields: "I wonder if ever, and how soon, I shall get a just estimate of how many jackasses there are in this ridiculous world." He was not seriously concerned. Had he not followed one masterpiece with another, and this in a single year?

A PICTURE OF A DECAYING HOUSE

In fact he had not quite done so. *The House of the Seven Gables* is his second-best book. Its charms are many, but Hawthorne was wrong when he told Bridge it was more characteristic of his mind, more proper and natural for him to write. The labor it involved was of a more pleasant sort, even if this meant care and thought; but the thought was not from the bottom of his mind. The "one tone" of *The Scarlet Letter* was the deepest, most dangerous, most painful tone he was ever to strike. It was natural for one of the two men in him—the man of the fancies and the sketches—to avoid striking it again, but it is tragic that this man succeeded. He succeeded in *The House of the Seven Gables* by lavishing all of his gift upon a picture. It was agreeable for Hawthorne to go patiently over the fine canvas he had found, and it will always be agreeable for readers to accompany him. A picture, notwithstanding, can never be a poem.

This picture is distinguished by the presence in it of one gaunt, unforgettable figure. Hepzibah Pyncheon might have been the result of Hawthorne's imagining what [his sister] Elizabeth would be like when she was old, assuming that her family was rich and had lived forever in a great house of their own. Hepzibah and her house have long outlived their meaning without having lost their power to move the beholder. The Pyncheon family is under a curse—not only the specific one laid upon it long ago by Matthew Maule, the victim of Colonel Pyncheon's cupidity [greed], but the more general one which Hawthorne for several years had been aware of whenever he considered, as he was pleased to do, the decay even in America, and indeed especially in America, of hereditary estates. It was a part of his democracy to do this, as in *The House of the Seven Gables* it was a part of it to correct the picture of Hepzibah and her house with dashes of new life in the form of Phoebe, an unspoiled country cousin, and Holgrave, a photographer who was counted on to represent in his modern ideas and his mechanical competence the coming age of America. Phoebe is the briskest and prettiest of Hawthorne's slight girls, and Holgrave—if only because of the way he opens the door for her after Judge Pyncheon's death—is worthy of her fresh, delightful person. But slight is what she is, and Holgrave never becomes clear, however eloquently Hawthorne writes sermons for him against the dead body of the past. Hawthorne is now trying to deal directly with the contemporary scene, and failing. He is trying to be a novelist, and he was never, at least in any familiar sense of the term, intended for one. Recognizing this, he slips back into romance—not into tragedy, where *The Scarlet Letter* had taken him, but into the sort of plot which permits Holgrave to be the last of the Maules, with an inherited talent for mesmerism, and which dictates that Judge Pyncheon shall die in the Dickens manner, his watch ticking longer than his heart does in a chair where Ralph Nickleby, [a character in Charles Dickens's novel *Nicholas Nickleby*,] and Mr. Pecksniff, [a character in Dickens's novel *Martin Chuzzlewit*,] might have sat as one man, his model. These things have the interest attaching to any ingenious plot, but ingenious plots were not the best thing Hawthorne was capable of. Lacking a great theme like that of *The Scarlet Letter*, he returns to his best here whenever he continues with the picture of Hepzibah and her house, and with the fainter, almost impalpable sketch he imposes upon it of Clifford, Hepzibah's pathetic brother, come back like a ghost from the prison where Judge Pyncheon sent him years ago.

PATHETIC CHARACTERS UNDER A CURSE

Phoebe first hears Clifford murmuring in the shadows of a room, and only gradually does she make out his figure there.

Perhaps it never emerges, though something very painful does when it appears that he cannot bear, as time goes on, the ugly face of his old sister. He is a worshipper of beauty; Hawthorne suspects all such men, and sees that we pity Hepzibah all the more. Our pity for her when she opened the cent-shop, and was so ashamed of that blot on her gentility, as well as of its ever-shocking bell, was mingled with amusement. There is no amusement now, as there is none in the great train-ride the brother and sister take together when they have forgotten being estranged by Hepzibah's unfortunate squint. The two of them, with their house and its famous chickens, those attenuated fowl over which Hawthorne went with so fine a pencil, are the substance of the book. If they do little but stand still while time decays, we have again a reminder that Hawthorne, having become a painter for the while, has in so far surrendered his command of moving stuff.

His preface sports with the idea that there may be a moral buried in the book for readers to find. "The wrongdoing of one generation lives into the successive ones, and, divesting itself of

---

TRANSFORMING A DULL SUBJECT

In The House of the Seven Gables, *Nathaniel Hawthorne creates characters with life and soul. Arthur Hobson Quinn, in* American Fiction: An Historical and Critical Survey, *credits Hawthorne with a descriptive style that gives beauty to an old house and its dull, ugly, and simple inhabitants.*

The House of the Seven Gables *has not the power of* The Scarlet Letter, *but it is a triumph again of Hawthorne's method of insight. What more unpromising material can be imagined than an old house, peopled by an ugly old maid, without friends, an invalid convict, a simple country girl, and a rather shadowy photographer? Yet Hawthorne invested these few figures with a deep and growing interest, not so much by their actions or conversations, as by the vivid narrative and descriptive touches, by the way he brings us into the inmost souls of the characters. He makes us see them, not by the process of dissection, but by making them transparent to our eyes. Above all, he charms us by the beauty which he has the power to draw from all things, human or inanimate, because he has put it there. . . . The moral of* The House of the Seven Gables *is clear enough. Evil will come out of evil, through many generations, but again it is not obtruded upon us.*

Arthur Hobson Quinn, *American Fiction: An Historical and Critical Survey.* New York: D. Appleton-Century, 1936.

every temporary advantage, becomes a pure and uncontrollable mischief." He at once denies this, as he insists that he has not written the book merely to "convince mankind—or, indeed, any one man—of the folly of tumbling down an avalanche of ill-gotten gold, or real estate, on the heads of an unfortunate posterity, thereby to maim and crush them, until the accumulated mass shall be scattered abroad in its original atoms." Yet he would like to have the words remembered, for he is not sure that his book is true if they are not true. He is still afraid of his "romantic improbabilities"—something which neither he nor any reader ever thought of in connection with *The Scarlet Letter*. *The Scarlet Letter* takes us beyond the limits of ordinary human nature, but only as tragedy does. Here in *The House of the Seven Gables*, when motion must be added to image, the best we can have is the hocus-pocus of a curse, and a mundane one at that. The deeds of *The Scarlet Letter* disturb the universe and reverberate to its darkest reaches. These deeds affect only one family's fortunes, and are crowned with happiness at last. Holgrave forgoes his modernity by marrying Phoebe and inheriting the estate. This conclusion is as feeble as the figure of Uncle Venner is. For even the main picture has its meager spots, and Uncle Venner [a character in *The House of the Seven Gables* who collects scraps for his pig] is the most pigment-thin of those.

THE MUSIC OF HAWTHORNE'S PROSE STYLE

The House of the Seven Gables, notwithstanding all this, deserves its high place among American narratives of any time. Its atmosphere haunts the memory long after details of action have been forgotten; for being of the second order, they are necessarily forgotten. It is "pervaded with that vague hum," as James has put it, "that indefinable echo, of the whole multitudinous life of man, which is the real sign of a great work of fiction." Then too, in the style, there steadily glow "those ingenious and meditative musings," says James once more, "rather melancholy . . . than joyous, which melt into the current of the story and give it a kind of moral richness." The prose of Hawthorne, an invisible weapon with which he can slay all but our toughest doubts, is with him a secret almost as deep as his moral richness, and doubtless it was born with that. In *The House of the Seven Gables* it not only glows but sounds. It is at once an inaudible weapon and the source of a music that moves us when nothing else does. "So much of mankind's varied experience had passed there—so much had been suffered, and something, too, enjoyed—that the very timbers were oozy, as with the moisture of a heart. It was itself like a great human heart, with a life of its own, and full of rich and sombre reminiscences." That is the house; and here is its chief inhabitant. "Forth she steps into the dusky, time-darkened passage; a tall figure, clad in black silk, with a long and shrunken waist, feeling her way towards the stairs like a near-sighted person, as in truth she is." Yet in no one sentence can the style of the book be wholly heard. It is everywhere and nowhere, like the feeling of its author. He has relaxed from *The Scarlet Letter* to enjoy a serener success. Not a saner one, for his wisdom among the Puritans, as someone has said, was that of a healthy man in a madhouse. But surely serener, for now he is in a curiosity shop, watching quaint personages of his own day.

One review of *The House of the Seven Gables* was written by a neighbor who lived six miles away, in Pittsfield. It purported to be an extract from the *Pittsfield Secret Review* but was in fact a letter—one of several great letters received by Hawthorne from this man. He was Herman Melville, whose brief blaze of friendship with Hawthorne is one of the major events in literary history. "We think the book," said Melville, "for pleasantness of running interest, surpasses the other works of the author. The curtains are more drawn; the sun comes in more; genialities peep out more." Hawthorne must have agreed with this, as he must have been pleased by the reviewer's praise of the picture he had painted—the book was called "a fine old chamber," abundantly furnished with "rich hangings wherein are braided scenes from tragedies." Melville was careful not to call *The House of the Seven Gables* itself a tragedy; he talked rather of its author's potentialities and implied powers. "We should like nothing better," he remarked, "than to devote an elaborate and careful paper to the full consideration and analysis of the purport and significance of what so strongly characterises all of this author's writings. There is a certain tragic phase of humanity which, in our opinion, was never more powerfully embodied than by Hawthorne. We mean the tragedies of human thought in its own unbiassed, native, and profounder workings. We think that into no recorded mind has the intense feeling of the usable truth ever entered more deeply than into this man's. By usable truth, we mean the apprehension of the absolute condition of present things as they strike the eye of the man who fears them not, though they do their worst to him. . . . There is the grand truth about Nathaniel Hawthorne. He says NO! in thunder; but the Devil himself cannot make him say yes. For all men who say yes, lie."

The Ambiguity of *The Scarlet Letter*

Richard Chase

Richard Chase explores the ambiguity of Nathaniel Hawthorne's *The Scarlet Letter* by presenting a range of viewpoints. The novel, he says, is a series of pictures, a mirror used to portray paradox, and a moral tale about sin and repentance. It is a feminist tract and a commentary on society and politics. He argues, however, that *The Scarlet Letter* is best seen as an "art-view of the world," a world of allegory and myth. While Chase provides the reader with his version of the book's allegorical symbols, he offers them tentatively, assuring the reader that the complexity of Hawthorne's work needs all of the interpretations for a deep understanding.

The Scarlet Letter has in abundance that "complexity of feeling" often attributed to the American novel. At the same time, the foreground elements of *The Scarlet Letter*—the salient actors and events—have something of the two-dimensionality of actors and events in legend. What baffles our best understanding is how to make the mysterious connections between the rather simple elements of the book and what is thought and felt about them. . . .

PICTURES, MIRRORS, AND MORALS

The Scarlet Letter is almost all picture. The adultery which sets everything going happens before the book begins, and it is never made believable. There are, to be sure, dramatic scenes—the three scenes on the scaffold; Hester and Pearl at the governor's mansion; Hester, Dimmesdale, and Pearl in the forest; and each of these scenes is exquisite and unforgettable.

Yet compared with the more immediate impact which in different hands they might have made on us, they seem frozen, muted, and remote. There is an abyss between these scenes and the reader, and they are like the events in a pageant or a dream, not like those of a stage drama. They are, in short, little differentiated from the pattern of the whole and they have the effect of being observed by the reader at second hand, of being reported to him, as in "picture." The author's powerfully possessive imagination refuses to relinquish his characters to our immediate perusal or to the logic of their own human destiny. This tight monolithic reticence is what gives *The Scarlet Letter* its unity and its mysterious remoteness. It is at every point the mirror of Hawthorne's mind, and the only one of his longer fictions in which we are not disturbed by the shortcomings of this mind but are content to marvel at its profound beauty.

Inevitably Hawthorne's symbol for the imagination was the mirror. [American critic and poet] Malcolm Cowley's account of the biographical origin of this idea seems correct. Cowley traces it to Hawthorne's sense of "doubleness," the result of a certain strain of narcissism and the long seclusion of Hawthorne's youth and young manhood. Temperamentally, as Cowley says, Hawthorne was paradoxically "cold and sensuous, sluggish and active, radical and conservative, and a visionary with a hard sense of money values." From this ingrained doubleness sprang Hawthorne's notion of the imagination. In the Introduction to *The Scarlet Letter*, for example, he uses the mirror to suggest that which gives frame, depth, and otherness to reality. His fictions are mirror-like. They give us a static and pictorial version of reality. They are uncanny and magical, but they capture little of life's drama, its emergent energy and warmth, its conflict, crisis, and catharsis. . . .

Some early readers of *The Scarlet Letter* believed not only that the subject was sin but that the author condoned sin, at least, the sin of adultery ("Is the French era actually begun in our literature?" cried one outraged reviewer). Certain later critics of Hawthorne have tended to agree that the author does condone sin, not because he was salacious but because, in his skeptical, secularized way, he was following the myth of "the fortunate fall," as [British poet John] Milton may be conceived to have done in *Paradise Lost.* Hawthorne certainly believed that no adulthood, no society, no tragic sense of life could exist without the knowledge of evil—a point he makes clear in the opening sentences of his book. Yet there seems to be no concerted myth of "the fortunate fall" in *The Scarlet Letter.*

What may be called the "grammar-school" idea of Hawthorne's novel supposes it to be a tale of sin and repentance. And this it certainly is, with strong stress on the repentance. More accurately, the subject of the book is the moral and psychological results of sin—the isolation and morbidity, the distortion and thwarting of the emotional life. From another point of view these are shown to be the results not of man's living in sin but of his living in a Puritan society, and thereby, to some extent, in any society. And yet it will not do to read *The Scarlet Letter* too closely as a comment on society, which is felt in its pages hardly more pervasively than sin.

FEMINISM AND POLITICS

To be sure there are elements of social comment in *The Scarlet Letter.* Is it not, for example, a feminist tract? So magically various is the book that one may sometimes think it is, even though a rich sensibility and profound mysteries are not usually associated with feminist literature. But doesn't Hester Prynne turn out to be rather like Hawthorne's sister-in-law Elizabeth Peabody, the emancipated reformer who became the prototype of Miss Birdseye in [American novelist Henry] James's *The Bostonians?* Once a luxurious and passionate woman, Hester takes up a life of renunciation and service. Her life turns "in a great measure from passion and feeling, to thought." In an age when "the human intellect" was "newly emancipated," she assumes "a freedom of speculation, then common enough on the other side of the Atlantic, but which our forefathers, had they known it, would have held to be a deadlier crime than that stigmatized by the scarlet letter." Thus, in her lonely life, Hester becomes a radical. She believes that sometime "a new truth" will be revealed and that "the whole relation between man and woman" will be established "on a surer ground of mutual happiness." She even comes to think in feminist rhetoric, and one can hear not only Hester but Miss Peabody and [New England feminist and writer] Margaret Fuller talking firmly about "the whole relation between man and woman."

Undoubtedly, then, *The Scarlet Letter* does have a feminist theme. It is even a tract, yet on the few occasions when it is heard the tractarian tone is tempered by the irony of the author. The book may have other meanings of a social or political kind. Still, one makes a mistake to treat Hawthorne, either in *The Scarlet Letter* or *The Blithedale Romance,* as if he were a political or social writer. He is a very canny observer of political fact, as of all fact, and this is in itself an unusual distinction. But no coherent politics is to be derived from Hawthorne. As [critic] Constance Rourke notes, Hawthorne seldom gives any strong impression of a society. *The Scarlet Letter* has, in Miss Rourke's words, "the bold and poetic and legendary outline which may belong to opera." In *The Scarlet Letter* and Hawthorne's other works the people at large are sensed merely as a choric crowd [a chorus] and the few main characters are rather artificially grouped in a village square, an old house, a shop, an isolated farm community, a forest glade, or a garden. The settings do not seem to be permanently related to each other or to the actors who momentarily speak their pieces in them.

In practice Hawthorne was an adherent of the mediocre [Franklin] Pierce wing of the Democratic party. Even less than Henry James had he any command over political theory or, what is more useful to a novelist, the instinct to dramatize politics in action. Hawthorne often gives the illusion of a systematic intellectual prowess, and this has led many readers to find in him an important moralist, political thinker, or theologian. It is an illusion, compounded of his hardheaded sagacity and his skepticism, his observance of elemental human truth. But the unities of his conceptions are first of all *aesthetic* unities, and Hawthorne tended to take an art-view of the world in so far as he took any consistent view at all. He stubbornly insisted that one could take such a view even in a democracy which appeared to have little use for aesthetic values.

ALLEGORY AND MYTH

Two other attitudes toward *The Scarlet Letter* must be noticed. [Poet and critic] Yvor Winters concludes that it is a "pure allegory" (as opposed to *The Blithedale Romance* and *The Marble Faun*, which Winters calls "novels with unassimilated allegorical elements"). Mr. Winters's discussion of Hawthorne includes a very instructive, if hardly exhaustive, account of the contradictory doctrines of New England Puritanism and of the allegorical sensibility these produced. He points out that the "Manicheistic struggle [a dualistic philosophy taught by the Persian prophet Manes] between Absolute Good and Absolute Evil," as conceived in early New England, was a rigid dualism that provided for a sense of two unalterably opposed and yet related orders of reality and that this dualism encouraged an allegorical habit of mind. He seems broadly correct in remarking that like a Puritan allegory the method of *The Scarlet Letter* is "neither narrative nor dramatic but expository."

If *The Scarlet Letter* is "pure allegory" then the symbols must by definition refer to fairly clear-cut and fixed referents. But of course they don't, and what we have in *The Scarlet Letter* is not pure allegory but a novel with (generally speaking) beautifully assimilated allegorical elements. This Mr. Winters seems indirectly to demonstrate by the unconvincing meanings he assigns to the characters—Hester representing the repentant sinner, Dimmesdale the half-repentant sinner, and Chillingworth the unrepentant sinner. . . .

As Mrs. [Q.D.] Leavis describes Hawthorne's "myth" [in her essay "Hawthorne as Poet,"] it is based on the ritual celebration of the historic transition from the "immemorial culture of the English folk with its Catholic and ultimately pagan roots" to the new Puritan consciousness. With some plausibility she discovers this myth in earlier pieces such as "The Maypole of Merrymount" and "My Kinsman, Major Molineux."

Hawthorne undeniably has the historical sense. And Mrs. Leavis might have gone on to observe that in "Mr. Higginbotham's Catastrophe" and *The House of the Seven Gables* we have in the careers of the rustic jacks-of-all-trade, Dominicus Pike and Holgrave, the succession of a capitalist order to an agrarian one. If she had seen this and other sides of Hawthorne's historical sense, Mrs. Leavis might have been more circumspect. She might have seen that there is no central unifying cultural "myth" in Hawthorne—only a clear perception of historical facts and an ability to endow these with beauty and significance. But the significance arises from the aesthetic harmonies of the composition as we find it from story to story, and although historical facts are observed, no theory or consistent view of history is presented.

Can we not make some kind of synthesis out of all these suggestions? We need some of their complexity. At the same time we have to remember that the simple truth about *The Scarlet Letter* is, as Constance Rourke said, that "Hawthorne was deeply engaged by the consideration of lost or submerged emotion." Let us add to this general formulation of the theme that *The Scarlet Letter* is an allegorical novel and that the allegory both in form and substance derives from Puritanism. Let us add, also, that although no unifying myth is involved, the novel describes the loss or submergence of emotion involved in the abandonment of the Old World cultural heritage which had given human emotions a sanction and a manifold significance.

Neither in *The Scarlet Letter* nor elsewhere did Hawthorne ever make up his mind whether he approved of this loss and submergence. Purely as an artist he often felt dismayed and discouraged by what Cooper called "the poverty of materials" which the workaday, uniform life of democracy had to offer. And on one side of his moral character, Hawthorne had enough passion to make us feel the sadness and chill of the New World—for example, when Hester Prynne lets her rich black hair loose in the forest sunshine but then with her meek masochism hides it again beneath the gray cap. At the same time, the other Hawthorne, the Puritan conventionalist, permits himself a sigh of relief and rationalizes it by reflecting that after all we are disillusioned now, after our passage from the Old World to the New, and if a certain beauty disappears along with licentiousness and sin, that is the price we pay for stern realism, our rectitude. and our practical sagacity.

If we are to hold to the idea that *The Scarlet Letter* is an allegory, we must assign meanings to the symbols of the story. This is an inviting prospect, but it has often led critics into very tedious speculations. As R. H. Fogle has said, there is generally speaking no special or exclusive symbolism in Hawthorne. His symbols are broadly traditional, coming to him from the Bible, Dante, [William] Shakespeare, Milton, [Edmund] Spenser, and [John] Bunyan—the light and the dark, the forest and the town, the dark woman and the fair woman, the fountain, the mirror, the cavern of the heart, the river, the sea, Eden, the rose, the serpent, fire and so on.

ALLEGORICAL SYMBOLS FOR HAWTHORNE'S PURPOSE

Within the context of these symbols, the allegory proper may be, however, more peculiar to Hawthorne. The allegorical symbols are Puritan categories revised for Hawthorne's own purposes, and they can be assigned provisionally in the following manner.

Hester Prynne, about whom there is something queenly, imperious, and barbaric, as well as fallible and appealing and enduring, represents the eternal woman, perhaps, indeed, the eternal human. When she puts on her gray cap and becomes a kind of social worker, her color and passion, her indeterminate, instinctual being is curbed and controlled. While this is going on Chillingworth and Dimmesdale are destroying each other. They are the two aspects of the will which confused Puritan thought in New England—the active and the inactive. From the beginning, Puritanism generated a strong belief in the efficacy of the will in overcoming all obstacles in the path of the New Israel in America, as in the path of the individual who strove toward Election [to be chosen by God for salvation]. But at the same time the doctrine of Predestination [the belief that God's plan is already determined] denied the possibility of any will except that of God.

Chillingworth unites intellect with will and coldly and with sinister motives analyzes Dimmesdale. This is the truly diabolic act in Hawthorne's opinion. It is what he calls the Unpardonable Sin and it is worse than sins of passions ("He has violated, in cold blood, the sanctity of a human heart," says Dimmesdale. "Thou and I, Hester, never did so!"). Hawthorne is as close a student of those impulses which drive men to plunder and exploit the human heart as [American novelist James Fenimore] Cooper and [American novelist William] Faulkner are of the impulses that drive men to plunder and exploit the land that Providence put into the trust of Americans. And for him as for them, violation, or impiety, is the worst of crimes.

Dimmesdale is intellect without will. He is passive; he is all eloquence, sensitivity, refinement, and moral scruple. What violence he has has long since been turned inward. He has preyed on himself as Chillingworth preys on him.

Little Pearl, one should say first, is a vividly real child whom Hawthorne modeled on his own little daughter Una. As a symbol as well as in life she is the offspring of Hester and an extension, as Hawthorne says, of the scarlet *A*. She represents the intuitive, lawless poetic view of the world. She is the eternal folk imagination, restored in every child, which is the fundamental element of the artist's imagination, and is outlawed by Puritan doctrine. "The spell of life went forth from her ever-creative spirit, and communicated itself to a thousand objects, as a torch kindles a flame wherever it may be applied." Ironically she conspires with everyone else in the tale to recreate the luxurious Hester in the puritan-democratic image. For it is she who insists that Hester shall replace the *A* and cover her hair with the gray cap.

As will be seen from the above, Chillingworth, Dimmesdale, and Pearl can be conceived as projections of different faculties of the novelist's mind—Chillingworth, the probing intellect; Dimmesdale, the moral sensibility; Pearl, the unconscious or demonic poetic faculty. Hester is the fallible human reality as the novelist sees it—plastic, various, inexhaustible, enduring, morally problematic.

From another point of view, we see that without becoming a myth, *The Scarlet Letter* includes several mythic archetypes.

The novel incorporates its own comic-book or folklore version. Chillingworth is the diabolical intellectual, perhaps even the mad scientist. Dimmesdale is the shining hero or to more sophisticated minds the effete New Englander. Hester is the scarlet woman, a radical and nonconformist, partly "Jewish" perhaps (there is at any rate an Old Testament quality about her, and Hawthorne says that her nature is "rich, voluptuous, Oriental." Like many other American writers, Hawthorne is not entirely above the racial folklore of the Anglo-Saxon peoples, which tends to depict tainted women and criminal men as French, Mediterranean, or Jewish—as in Hawthorne's *Marble Faun*, Miriam is Jewish, in Melville's *Pierre* Isabel is French, and in *Billy Budd* Claggart is dimly Mediterranean). Pearl is sometimes reminiscent of Little Red Riding Hood or a forest sprite of some sort who talks with the animals. Later when she inherits a fortune and marries a foreign nobleman, she is the archetypal American girl of the international scene, like the heroines of [William Dean] Howells and James. The subculture from which these discordant archetypes emerge is evidently inchoate [imperfectly formed or developed] and derivative. The symbols do not cohere until they have been made into projections of the faculties of the artist's mind and elements of a quasi-puritan allegory. But to a receptive imagination, they connect *The Scarlet Letter* with universal folklore, as many other novels, good and bad, are connected.

Old and New Worlds in *The Scarlet Letter*

Michael Davitt Bell

Michael Davitt Bell writes that Nathaniel Hawthorne contrasts Old England and New England in *The Scarlet Letter*. Hawthorne makes reference to the homes, heraldry, and fashion of England in the seventeenth century, and presents Hester Prynne and her decorated *A* and Pearl, Hester's daughter, in her elaborate clothing as symbols of Old World passion and refinement. At the end of the book, Bell notes, Hester sacrifices her rich, passionate nature to become an American. Ironically, Pearl, born in New England, moves abroad and retains her Old World richness.

The action of the *The Scarlet Letter* takes place entirely in a small New World settlement at the edge of a wilderness, far from the court and aristocracy of Old England. Thus the book's closing emphasis on heraldry, the symbolism of aristocracy, seems a bit curious. It may be appropriate that Pearl, who has apparently married into some noble continental family, should send her mother "letters . . . with armorial seals upon them, though of bearings unknown to English heraldry." But the closing paragraph, describing Hester's tomb in the Boston graveyard, applies heraldry to the New World as well:

> All around, there were monuments carved with armorial bearings; and on this simple slab of slate—as the curious investigator may still discern, and perplex himself with the purport— there appeared the semblance of an engraved escutcheon [a shield-shaped emblem]. It bore a device, a herald's wording of which might serve for a motto and brief description of our now concluded legend; so sombre is it, and relieved only by one ever-glowing point of light gloomier than the shadow:—

> "ON A FIELD, SABLE, THE LETTER A, GULES."
> [In heraldry the color red]

The peculiar relevance of this ending to the romance as a

From Michael Davitt Bell, *Hawthorne and the Historical Romance of New England*; Copyright ©1971 by Princeton University Press. Reprinted by permission of Princeton University Press.

whole can be seen if one turns back, briefly, to the opening scene—Hester's exposure on the scaffold. In the midst of her humiliation Hester's mind wanders to recollections of her old home in England. She recalls her infancy, her mother, her "father's face, with its bald brow, and reverend white beard, that flowed over the old-fashioned Elizabethan ruff [a ruffled collar]." Of particular interest is her recollection of "her native village, in Old England, and her paternal home; a decayed house of gray stone, with a poverty-stricken aspect, but retaining a half-obliterated shield of arms over the portal, in token of antique gentility." *The Scarlet Letter* chronicles Hester's movement from a heraldry of the Old World to a heraldry of the New—from a "token of antique gentility" to a token better suited to symbolize life in New England. Between the decaying home in England and the stark gravestone in the wilderness is a change from Old World to New that permeates the entire book.

The nature of this change is made clear in the brief first chapter of *The Scarlet Letter.* "The founders of a new colony," writes Hawthorne, "whatever Utopia [an ideal state, socially, politically, and morally] of human virtue and happiness they might originally project, have invariably recognized it among their earliest practical necessities to allot a portion of the virgin soil as a cemetery, and another portion as the site of a prison." Idealism gives way to practicality. The contrast between idealism and grim practicality is picked up, in this chapter, in the contrast between the rosebush that grows beside the prison door and the prison itself, "the black flower of civilized society." This contrast is continued through the rest of the romance. Few readers of *The Scarlet Letter* miss the opposition in the book between scarlet and gray, between the passionate, feminine values associated with Hester and the severe, masculine values of the Puritan society.

HESTER AND PEARL REPRESENT THE OLD WORLD

It is important to note further, however, that Hawthorne associates the rosebush, Hester, the scarlet letter, and even Hester's needlework, not only with feminine passion or with a richer ideal of life but also (like roses in so many of his stories) with the values of the Old World as opposed to those of the New. Thus Hester, when she first appears, is not simply a woman of an "impulsive and passionate nature." Her magnificent clothes, noteworthy only because she is wearing them in Boston, are of the more lavish British fashion. She is specifically compared to a Catholic painting of the Virgin. Even her ornamentation of the scarlet letter is described as exemplifying a skill "of which the dames of a court might gladly have availed themselves." When Hester denies her passionate side in order to survive in the New World, it is important to note that it is also her European side that she is denying. The great moment in the forest when Hester lets down her hair and regains her passionate beauty occurs only after she and Dimmesdale have determined to return to England. The "scarlet" side of Hester's character cannot survive in New England.

If Hester does pass on the qualities represented by the rose-

---

GOVERNOR BELLINGHAM EMULATES OLD ENGLAND

In the chapter of Nathaniel Hawthorne's The Scarlet Letter *entitled "The Governor's Hall," Hester and Pearl deliver embroidered gloves to Governor Bellingham at his mansion. Hawthorne describes the mansion in detail with several references to English elegance.*

Governor Bellingham had planned his new habitation after the residences of gentlemen of fair estate in his native land. Here, then, was a wide and reasonably lofty hall, extending through the whole depth of the house. . . . The furniture of the hall consisted of some ponderous chairs, the backs of which were elaborately carved with wreaths of oaken flowers; and likewise a table in the same taste; the whole being of the Elizabethan age, or perhaps earlier, and heirlooms, transferred hither from the Governor's paternal home. On the table—in token that the sentiment of old English hospitality had not been left behind—stood a large pewter tankard, at the bottom of which, had Hester or Pearl peeped into it, they might have seen the frothy remnant of a recent draught of ale.

On the wall hung a row of portraits, representing the forefathers of the Bellingham lineage, some with armour on their breasts, and others with stately ruffs and robes of peace. All were characterized by the sternness and severity which old portraits so invariably put on; as if they were the ghosts, rather than the pictures, of departed worthies, and were gazing with harsh and intolerant criticism at the pursuits and enjoyments of living men.

At about the centre of the oaken panels, that lined the hall, was suspended a suit of mail, not, like the pictures, an ancestral relic, but of the most modern date; for it had been manufactured by a skilful armorer in London, the same year in which Governor Bellingham came over to New England.

Nathaniel Hawthorne, *The Scarlet Letter*, 1850.

bush or the scarlet letter, it is through her daughter, Pearl. Hester deliberately represents, in the elaborate clothing she sews for Pearl, "the scarlet letter in another form." But the characteristics of Pearl are not transmitted to the character of New England in general. It is one of the curious features of *The Scarlet Letter* that Pearl, the only important character born in New England, is continually associated with Europe and eventually leaves New England to settle there. Pearl's association with the Old World is clear in the visit she and her mother pay to the mansion of Governor Bellingham—a scene in which Hawthorne is very much concerned with the tension in New England between the values of Old World and New. Bellingham's mansion clearly represents an attempt to reproduce in the New World the values of the Old. At the door Hester and Pearl are greeted by a servant who, we are told, "wore the blue coat, which was the customary garb of serving-men at that period, and long before, in the old hereditary halls of England." "Governor Bellingham," writes Hawthorne, "had planned his new habitation after the residences of gentlemen of fair estate in his native land." The costume of Bellingham himself, when he appears, is dominated by "the wide circumference of an elaborate ruff, beneath his gray beard, in the antiquated fashion of King James's reign," [king of England who followed Elizabeth I] recalling Hester's memory on the scaffold of "her father's face, with its bald brow, and reverend white beard, that flowed over the old-fashioned Elizabethan ruff."

OLD AND NEW WORLD NATURE

The garden, too, represents an attempt to transplant the values of the Old World. But here we see that such an attempt is doomed to failure. "The proprietor," we are told, "appeared already to have relinquished, as hopeless, the effort to perpetuate on this side of the Atlantic, in a hard soil and amid the close struggle for subsistence, the native English taste for ornamental gardening." Bellingham's attempt at an English garden is being overrun by pumpkins and cabbages. There are a few apple trees and rosebushes, but these, significantly, were planted by the Anglican Blackstone, the "flower-decked priest" of "The Maypole of Merry-Mount." And, to return to my original point, it is with the roses, not the pumpkins, that Pearl identifies. She cries for a rose when she first sees the garden, and when the Reverend Mr. Wilson asks her who made her she "announced," so Hawthorne writes, "that she had not been made at all, but had been plucked by her mother off the bush of wild roses, that grew by the prison door." Pearl's association with Old England is not only symbolic. Bellingham, seeing her, is reminded of the court masks of the time of King James, of those called "the children of the Lord of Misrule." Wilson is reminded of stained-glass windows and pagan superstitions. "Methinks," he declares, "I have seen just such figures, when the sun has been shining through a richly painted window, and tracing out the golden and crimson images across the floor. But that was in the old land. . . . Art thou a Christian child,—ha? Dost know thy catechism? Or art thou one of those naughty elfs or fairies, whom we thought to have left behind us, with other relics of Papistry, in merry old England?" "I am mother's child," answers Pearl.

It might be objected that this picture of Pearl as European obscures the fact that she is the child of "nature," at home in the forest or on the seashore. To this I can only answer that for Hawthorne nature itself is more a part of the European character than of the American. "Nature" and the Old World are both comprehended, for Hawthorne, in the notion of the pagan—in the easy, permissive religion of "merry Old England" as opposed to the stern, repressive religion of New England. Thus in "The Maypole of Merry-Mount" the forces of nature are represented, not by the Puritans but by the Anglican revelers. Hawthorne seems to have dissented from the popular belief that the proximity of the wilderness led to the growth of a "natural" American character. On the contrary, he seems to say, the first settlers were too close to nature to be "natural." "Nature" for them was not a rose garden but a wilderness, not a pastoral masque [a play performed by masked players] but an Indian massacre. Both nature and Europe represented a threat to the stability of the new enterprise, and it is not always an easy matter to distinguish the part of each in the overall danger. Chillingworth has learned his black arts both from European scholars and wild Indians. It is almost indifferent to Hester, in considering escape from the restrictions of the Puritans, whether that escape be to the freedom of Europe or to the freedom of the wilderness. And finally, to return to my original point, Pearl is at home both in the forest and in Europe.

THE EFFECT OF THE NEW WORLD ON WOMEN

The point is, with all due emphasis on the word "home," that Pearl is *not* at home in Boston. Her apparent disappearance to the continent at the close simply makes more explicitly the point made by the defeminizing of her mother—namely, that certain qualities of richness and passion, both natural and European, did not long survive the migration to New England. At the beginning of the opening scene of *The Scarlet Letter* Hawthorne comments on the changes that have taken place in New England women since the time of the first settlers:

> Morally, as well as materially, there was a coarser fibre in these wives and maidens of Old English birth and breeding, than in their fair descendants, separated from them by a series of six or seven generations; for, throughout that chain of ancestry, every successive mother has transmitted to her child a fainter bloom, a more delicate and briefer beauty, and a slighter physical frame, if not a character of less force and solidity, than her own.

Pearl is no part of this historical progression toward a "fainter bloom." Throughout all her character "there was a trait of passion, a certain depth of hue, which she never lost; and if, in any of her changes, she had grown fainter or paler, she would have ceased to be herself;—it would have been no longer Pearl!" As surely as the death of Ilbrahim in "The Gentle Boy" the removal of Pearl at the end of *The Scarlet Letter* signifies a narrowing or limitation of possibilities in the growth of the American character. Hester must choose at the close between Europe and America—between living with her daughter abroad or returning to Boston. She chooses the latter and her choice requires the sacrifice of a whole side of her character. As in "Endicott and the Red Cross" or "The Maypole of Merry-Mount" so here, too, the price of independence is loss. Even on the scaffold, in the opening scene, Hester is aware that she can never return to the Old World, that her identity must now be adapted to the conditions of her New World: her isolation, her child, the scarlet *A* on her breast. "Yes!" we are told of her thoughts "—these were her realities,—all else had vanished!" In coming to terms with her "realities" Hester comes to terms with the conditions of life in the wilderness. In *The Scarlet Letter* (and one might speculate on further meanings for the initial *A*) Hester Prynne becomes, quite simply, an American.

Color and Light Images in *The Scarlet Letter*

Hyatt Howe Waggoner

Hyatt Howe Waggoner analyzes the color and light images in Nathaniel Hawthorne's *The Scarlet Letter.* He classifies the images into three categories: pure (literal uses of color), mixed (images with both literal and figurative meaning), and drained (images with only figurative meaning). Waggoner presents each category with numerous examples. He goes on to explain that the three types of images gain meaning by their association with natural good, moral good, natural evil, and moral evil. According to Waggoner, Hawthorne played the colors and shades of light off of one another to give them the status of "actors in the story."

In the three short paragraphs that make up his opening chapter Hawthorne introduces the three chief symbols that will serve to give structure to the story on the thematic level, hints at the fourth, and starts two of the chief lines of imagery. The opening sentence suggests the darkness ("sad-colored," "gray"), the rigidity ("oak," "iron"), and the aspiration ("steeple-crowned") of the people "amongst whom religion and law were almost identical." Later sentences add "weather-stains," "a yet darker aspect," and "gloomy" to the suggestions already begun through color imagery. The closing words of the chapter make the metaphorical use of color explicit: Hawthorne hopes that a wild rose beside the prison door may serve "to symbolize some sweet moral blossom, that may be found along the track, or relieve the darkening close of a tale of human frailty and sorrow.". . .

The extremes of Mr. Wilson's "light" and Chillingworth's "blackness" meet not only in the gray of Hester's dress and the Puritan hats, and in the indeterminate drabness of the Puritan clothing, but also in the ambiguous suggestions of red. Images

Reprinted by permission of the publisher from *Hawthorne: A Critical Study* by Hyatt Howe Waggoner (Cambridge, MA: Harvard University Press), copyright ©1955, 1963 by the President and Fellows of Harvard College.

of color, and of light and shade, are more numerous than any other images in the novel. Readers have always been aware that Hawthorne has used these images "artistically," and sometimes that he has used them "expressively"; yet precisely what they express and how they express it have never, even in the extended treatments of the subject, been adequately analyzed. Some of them Hawthorne makes explicitly symbolic, others seem obscurely to be so, while still others resist every effort at translation into abstract terms. . . . I think it will prove useful as a preliminary to later analysis to distinguish among three ways in which images of color and light and shade appear in the novel.

There is, first, the pure sensory image used literally [with exact meaning, factual], not figuratively [based on figures of speech, metaphorical], though the literalness of its use will not destroy whatever intrinsic symbolic value it may have. Second, there is the color or shade of light or darkness that must be taken literally but that also has explicit symbolic value. Finally, there is the image that has only, or chiefly, symbolic value, so that it cannot be taken literally. I shall call these pure, mixed, and drained images. . . .

PURE, MIXED, AND DRAINED IMAGES

On the first page the grayness of the hats and the "weather-stains" of the jail are pure images, sense impressions to be taken quite literally. Only after we have become conscious of the part played by color in the tale are we apt to be aware of the appropriateness of these colors, though to be sure they may have had their effect on us before we became conscious of that effect. So likewise the "bright" morning sun and the "ruddy" cheeks of the spectators in the next chapter are first of all, and always fundamentally, to be understood in a perfectly literal sense. Again, the first time the scarlet letter is mentioned, the color image is pure: "On the breast of her gown, in fine red cloth, surrounded with an elaborate embroidery and fantastic flourishes of gold-thread, appeared the letter *A*."

Mixed images, on the other hand, have more than that suggestion of figurative extension that any image, however pure, will have: they may be said to *denote* [to signify directly] both literal and figurative colors, so that in them the natural symbolism of color becomes explicit. The jail is "gloomy," that is, both physically and emotionally dark. The second time the letter is mentioned, its color has acquired a moral connotation [having a suggested meaning] from its context: Hester stood before the crowd with "desperate recklessness" while everyone looked at the sign of her ignominy, "that SCARLET LETTER." More clearly an example of this mixed type of image is the beadle's [a minor parish official's] statement that here in this righteous colony "iniquity is dragged out into the sunshine": for Hester has just been brought from the literal darkness of the jail into the literal sunshine of the square, and this action is an example of "iniquity" which has been hidden or unknown being made public, brought into the (figurative) light. The speaker has meant his remark as a figure of speech, while the reader sees that it is literally appropriate too; there is a two-way movement, from the literal to the figurative, and from the figurative back to the literal, going on here and elsewhere in the color images in the novel. One final example in this preliminary survey of the mixed type of image: "his face darkened with some powerful emotion." Now powerful emotion may literally darken the face by flushing it, but here the symbolic effect of darkness, as that which is feared and evil, is also clear. This is the first reference to the "darkness" of Chillingworth.

The third or drained type of image is much less frequent than the other two. (There are ten times as many pure images as drained, and about twice as many mixed, according to my count.) On the first page we hear of the "black flower" of civilized society, a prison, and we realize that "black" is here figurative, for though the jail has been described as dark and weatherstained, it is not black in any literal sense. Again, in the last sentence of the first chapter we hear of the "darkening close" of the tale, and we read "darkening" to mean gloomy (in the emotional sense), sad. Finally, when the Reverend Mr. Wilson speaks to Hester of the "blackness" of her sin, the primary significance of the word, both for Hester and for the reader, is intensive and qualitative in a moral sense; the residue of literal meaning merely adds to the emotional overtones. Here, as in the "smile of dark and self-relying intelligence" displayed by Chillingworth, there is hardly any literal meaning left.

THE MEANING OF COLOR AND LIGHT

The colors presented in these three types of images are associated with natural good (beauty, health), moral and spiritual good (holiness), natural evil (ugliness, death), and moral evil (sin). With the exception of the yellow starch on the linen of Mistress Hibbens, in which I can discern only historical verisimilitude [appearing to be true or real], all the colors in

HEART IMAGES IN *THE SCARLET LETTER*

The heart is a frequently recurring image in Nathaniel Hawthorne's The Scarlet Letter. *Hyatt H. Waggoner, who analyzes heart images as well as color and light images in* Hawthorne: A Critical Study, *identifies the heart as a prison, a dungeon, a hearth, a grave, and a forest.*

There are nearly twice as many heart images as there are flower and weed images, but with one exception Hawthorne insists upon them less. If they are in some respects even more revealing, we may guess that that is because they spring from Hawthorne's deepest concerns and most abiding insights, not from the top of his head but from his own heart. . . .

The most extended heart image is the forest scene. The forest in which Hester and Pearl take their walk has all the attributes common to normal human hearts in Hawthorne's work. It is black, mysterious, dismal, dim, gloomy, shadowy, obscure, and dreary. It is thought by the public to be where the Black Man meets his accomplices. It has in its depths a stream which as it mirrors the truth whispers "tales out of the heart of the old forest." But when Hester and Dimmesdale decide to follow the dictates of their hearts and, escaping man's law, live by nature, then "the wood's heart of mystery" becomes a "mystery of joy" and sunshine lights up the gloomy spot. In the four chapters concerned with this meeting, heart imagery plays a leading part, so that no analysis of the incident is likely to be adequate which does not take it into account.

Hyatt H. Waggoner, *Hawthorne: A Critical Study.* Rev. ed. Cambridge, MA: The Belknap Press of Harvard University Press, 1971.

the novel, including yellow as used elsewhere, are associated with one or more natural or moral values, positive or negative. The most frequent colors are red in its several shades and black, pure or mixed, as in "gray," "shadowy," and "darksome." Red is ambiguous throughout, suggesting both sunlight and roses, on the one hand, and the traditional associations called up by "the scarlet woman" on the other. Pearl, a "natural" child, is dressed in red, Hester's letter is red, the roses are red, the bloom on healthy cheeks is red, and the glow in Chillingworth's eyes is thought to be red with the light of infernal fires. Black, dark gray, brown, all the darker shades, ordinarily suggest both natural and moral evil. Green and yellow are associated with natural good, with life and beauty.

Light is of various kinds. Sunlight suggests both truth and health. It is analogous to the spiritual Light of Revelation, which in Hawthorne's scheme of values should "illumine" nature, and to the light of grace. But there are also the "false light" of meteors and the "red light" of evil. Mr. Wilson, the most saintly of the Puritan ministers and the most sympathetic of the lesser characters, has "white" hair and light-colored ("gray") eyes, in marked contrast to the only colors assigned to Governor Bellingham, who has a "dark" feather and a "black" tunic. Thus too Dimmesdale, a mixed figure of lofty aspirations and base conduct, is seen as having a "white," lofty, and impending brow and "brown," melancholy eyes. Dressed in "black," he walks by choice in the "shadowy" bypaths. Hester is seen as red (her letter and her vivid complexion), gray (her dress), and black (her hair and eyes), the first two ambiguous in their associations, the last saved from being wholly negative by the glints of sunlight often seen in her hair. Pearl, though she has her mother's black hair and eyes, is usually seen as a flash of red and light: the "deep and vivid tints" of her "bright" complexion and "gorgeous robes" often throw an absolute circle of "radiance" around her. Chillingworth is compounded of shades of "darkness," except for the red, or reddish blue, glow thought to be seen in his eyes.

RHYTHMIC, FUNCTIONAL, EXPRESSIVE COLOR

The relationships between the three types of images, the several colors, and their associated moral and natural values are highly complex, but I shall risk a few generalizations, the first of which is the most obvious. The use of colors in the novel is rhythmic, but it is more than that, for the rhythm is functional and expressive. In "The Interior of a Heart," for instance, there are twenty-two color images, all but two of which are black or white. The heart is Dimmesdale's, and Dimmesdale wavers between good and evil, we might almost say between the supernatural and the unnatural. It is conceptually right that he should be associated with both the radiance of Wilson and the darkness of Chillingworth. He is never associated with the greens and yellows and reds of sunlit nature.

Again, the chapter called "Hester at Her Needle" has eighteen color images, eleven of them red, seven black, dark, and white. Hester stands in an ambiguous position between Chillingworth and the white maidens, as Dimmesdale does between Chillingworth and Wilson, but she differs from him in her relation to nature. For a final example, on one page of "The Minister's Vigil," when the approach of Mr. Wilson and the threat of disclosure coincide, there are nine color images, eight of which are of light or whiteness. Recalling the beadle's earlier remark about the Puritan effort to drag iniquity out into the sunshine, in which light was associated with an uncharitable violation of the human heart, we become aware of what is sometimes obscured in discussions of Hawthorne: that color imagery is functional *in context*, not static or determined by some abstract scheme.

The most significant use of color in the novel is in the three key scenes, Hester on the scaffold with the infant Pearl, Dimmesdale with Hester and Pearl on the scaffold at midnight, and the three on the scaffold again at the end. In the first, Hester is dragged into the light and stands there "with the hot, mid-day sun burning down upon her face, and lighting up its shame; with the scarlet token of infamy on her breast. . ." In the second there is at first only the darkness of the "obscure night," which renders Dimmesdale's gesture ineffectual. Then two kinds of light appear. First there is the gleam of the lantern of the saintly Mr. Wilson, who appeared in his illuminated circle to be radiant with the "distant shine of the celestial city"; but Mr. Wilson's light does not reach Dimmesdale, who is thus "saved" by a narrow margin from disclosure. After Mr. Wilson's light recedes in the darkness, a meteor flames in the sky, making all visible, but in a "false" light, so that what Chillingworth sees by its aid is not true. Neither light in this scene accomplishes the necessary revelation. That is left for the final climactic scaffold scene, in which the three come together voluntarily in the light of the sun.

IMAGES ACCUMULATE MEANING

The second generalization I should like to suggest about the light and color images is this: their significance is enriched by the relations between the three types of images. In the first place, the pure images are so much the most numerous that they tend to establish, by sheer weight of repetition, the reading of the others. Where there is so much blackness, "gloomy" is bound to carry its physical as well as its emotional denotation. This becomes clearer when we compare the use of darkness in, say, *Dr. Grimshawe's Secret* with its use here. When in the later novel Redclyffe is said to exist in a darkened dream, we do not know quite what to make of it, for darkness has not been established as a motif [a recurring element] in the novel. But when Governor Bellingham says that Pearl is "in the dark" concerning her soul, the expression means far more to the reader than that she is not, in the opinion of the governor, properly instructed: it calls up the whole range of colors, and the moral and other values attached to them, which the reader has absorbed by this time. We have another of those sudden expansions from image to symbol that is so conspicuous a feature of the novel.

In short, the marked predominance of pure images keeps the mixed and drained ones from losing force by becoming abstractly figurative, and this in turn is one of the reasons why the novel never becomes allegory. Though we must say that there is a struggle going on in the novel between the forces of darkness and of light, the preponderance of pure images keeps this struggle from becoming neatly dichotomous [divided into contradictory parts]. When we read that Chillingworth had conceived "a new purpose, dark, it is true, if not guilty," we do not read this as a pleonasm[redundancy, repetition], for darkness has acquired many associations beyond the guilt it may hide. Again, the "light" of the church is saved from being a mere figure for "the teaching of the church" by the fact that light has become associated with a cluster of positive values, both natural and moral, that cannot be translated adequately as "doctrine."

Finally, two drained images will illustrate the point. "The holy whiteness of the clergyman's good fame," in reference to Dimmesdale, draws a part of its meaning from the light constantly associated with Mr. Wilson and Christian Revelation, but another part from the false light of the meteor, which has only recently ceased to cast its distorting glare over the scene. And the smile that "flickered" over Chillingworth's face "so derisively" that the spectator could see his "blackness" "all the better for it" is also a false light which nevertheless may reveal some things truly, as the light of the meteor had revealed "the black, freshly turned earth" of the garden plots near the scaffold.

But the movement flows in another direction too, for the presence of the mixed and drained images underlines the symbolic value of the pure images. When Pearl, inspired by her mother's example, makes a letter out of eelgrass for her own breast, and Hester says that "the green letter, and on thy childish bosom, has no purport," we realize that the statement is true in several different senses: from Hester's point of view, the green letter has none of the "purport" that her own letter has, and she, of course, is preoccupied with just that kind of meaning; but from the reader's point of view, the greenness of the letter is an appropriate reminder of Pearl's association with nature. And when we see the Indians in the square on Election Day, the predominant reds and yellows of their barbaric finery and the black of their "snakelike" eyes carry associations with nature and with evil, but none at all with "celestial illumination." Like the weathered wood of the jail, the Indian costumes gather meaning from their context.

COLORS MOVE BACK AND FORTH

The point of my third generalization about the three types of images has perhaps already become sufficiently clear from what has been said, but it is so important that I should not like to let it rest on implication. The movement of the different colors back and forth between pure and drained images helps to keep what Hawthorne calls his "mesh of good and evil" a true mesh, with the strands intricately interwoven. Hawthorne usually presents a pure image first, establishing the sensed color, then expands it into a mixed image, exploring its connotations, then at last uses the color in a drained image that out of the total context of the novel would be bare and lifeless, or merely whimsical, but that in context is rich in the associations it has acquired along the way. But sometimes he reverses this process, and sometimes he jumbles the order, so that the colors are never completely fixed in the degree of their literalness or the extension of their symbolic values. When we read, for instance, of the "radiant halo" surrounding the head of Mr. Wilson as he walked through a "gloomy night of sin," the image that we should expect to be merely figurative, the "halo" of sanctity, turns out to be literal as well, for the light is shed by Mr. Wilson's lantern; and the one that we should at first expect to be literal—for we already know that it is a dark night, and as we start reading "this gloomy night . . ." we think we are getting a mere restatement of the darkness—turns out to be also figurative, forcing us to revise the reaction we had prepared.

The relations between the light and color images and their symbolic values are, then, neither static and schematized nor wholly free and arbitrary, but contextual within a general framework supplied by traditional patterns of color symbolism. The traditional associations of light and dark, for example, are apparently archetypal. Literature is filled with the darkness of death and sin and the light of life and goodness; and the common speech allows us to "throw light" upon a problem as often as we "explain" or "clarify" it. Perhaps the most nearly fixed in its symbolic values of all the colors in the novel is black. Yet even it is sometimes used ambiguously. Hester's black hair, that glistened so often in the sunlight before she covered it with a cap, and Pearl's "dark, glistening curls," so well set off by her scarlet costume, are examples. On the other hand, the red that runs through the book as a motif is almost always used ambiguously. Only a few examples, like the "red glare" in Chillingworth's eyes, are wholly clear, with one set of suggestions canceled out and another emphasized. The wild roses and the scarlet letter, Pearl's costume and her mother's complexion do not exhaust the possibilities. Chillingworth's light is thought to be a reflection of the infernal fires, but Pearl is also said to be a flame. When the forest, seeming to recognize a kindred spirit in Pearl, offers her partridgeberries "red as drops of blood" the gift carries with it memories not only of the rose bush but of the scarlet letter.

COLORS AS ACTORS

In short, red, black, gray, sunlight, firelight, and the less frequent green, yellow, blue, and purple are not simply descriptive of the setting and characters. In a very real sense they are themselves actors in the story that moves through and behind the story. Even in their absence they help to tell the tale. When we find that the most strongly and frequently presented colors are those most commonly associated with negative or ambiguous moral values, or with positive natural values, and that the light of positive moral and spiritual values is both less vivid and less frequent, we are not surprised. The first chapter prepared us for this. Perhaps the largest generalization we may draw from a study of the approximately 425 light and color images is that Hawthorne conceived, but when writing the novel did not strongly feel, the possibility of escape from evil and the past.

History, Art, and Wisdom in *The Scarlet Letter*

Randall Stewart and Dorothy Bethurum

Randall Stewart and Dorothy Bethurum argue that Nathaniel Hawthorne's *The Scarlet Letter* is "a historical novel" because it portrays early New England Puritanism with accuracy. But, they maintain, it is also a work of art with a carefully crafted plot and powerful symbolic language. Hawthorne uses a local ordinance from Boston's early days to advance his own themes of the human heart. Because he explores human relationships that apply to all people regardless of time or place, his themes have universal appeal.

Nathaniel Hawthorne was the chief inheritor, in literature, of the New England Puritan tradition, and *The Scarlet Letter* is the epitome of that inheritance. More truly than any other book in American literature, *The Scarlet Letter* embodies Puritan ideals and the Puritan way of life. It is, therefore, an important historical document. But it is more than that, for Hawthorne's treatment of his subject achieves, by means of allegory and symbolism, meanings that are universally applicable to human life.

A HISTORICAL NOVEL

Hawthorne knew well the early history of New England and used it repeatedly as a source of literary material. His first American ancestor, William Hathorne, came over from England with John Winthrop in 1630, and later, as a magistrate of the Massachusetts Bay Colony, ordered the public whipping of a Quakeress. William's son, John, was a member of the Salem court that, in 1692, condemned to death those convicted of witchcraft. Hawthorne felt deeply his connection with these forebears. In the autobiographical essay "The Custom House," he spoke of himself as "their representative," and went on to say, "I hereby take shame upon myself for their sakes, and pray that any curse incurred by them . . . may be now and henceforth removed." Despite his disapproval of their bigotry and cruelty, he recognized the ancestral tie: "Strong traits of their nature," he said, "have intertwined themselves with mine." It might not be farfetched to think that the writing of *The Scarlet Letter* was, for Hawthorne, a kind of expiation of his ancestors' guilt. But whether this be true or not, few books have come so completely out of the inherited experience of the author.

The Scarlet Letter is, in a sense, a historical novel. The plot is the author's invention, and the four chief characters—Arthur Dimmesdale, Hester Prynne, Roger Chillingworth, Pearl—are fictitious per sons. But the lesser characters—Governor Bellingham, the Reverend John Wilson, Mistress Hibbins, Master Brackett, the jailer—are historical figures prominent in the early annals of Boston. Details of setting and costume are faithfully rendered. The reader can assume that Mistress Hibbins' elaborate headdress, for example, is historically accurate; likewise, the market place, whose conspicuous features are the meeting house, the jail, and the scaffold; accurate, too, the ceremonies accompanying the Election Sermon, and the pervasive allusions to witchcraft; for Hawthorne was something of a research scholar in colonial New England history. Moreover, the plot itself, though invented, is based upon a historical form of punishment: Plymouth Colony, for example, passed a law in 1636 requiring that anyone guilty of adultery should "weare two Capitall letters viz. AD. cut out in cloth and sowed on theire upermost Garments on theire arme or backe; and if att any time they shalbee taken without the said letters whiles they are in the Gov'ment soe worn to bee forthwith taken and publickly whipt." Historians, in general, have made no objection to *The Scarlet Letter* as a picture of mid-seventeenth century Boston, except the qualification that the historical reality was probably somewhat less somber than Hawthorne's representation. If Hawthorne overemphasized the somberness, the reason is seen in the artistic fitness of such an emphasis in a "drama of guilt and sorrow": Hawthorne was a creative artist as well as a historian.

The Scarlet Letter is remarkable, among other things, for its tight, unified structure. The unity is not of the kind imposed by a single character: there is no chief character, no character who monopolizes the reader's attention and dominates the action throughout. The unity of the book is, rather, a complex one that grows out of the interactions between the characters.

And there is everywhere a perfect correspondence between character and incident: everywhere character determines incident, and incident illustrates character.

THE COMMUNITY'S FORCE

The action of *The Scarlet Letter* may be divided into four phases [according to the analysis of John C. Gerber]. In the first phase (Chapters 1–8), the community supplies the force necessary to set the story in motion. Hester is required by the community to wear the scarlet letter and to stand in ignominy on the scaffold. Community pressure, too, is the occasion of Chillingworth's visit to Hester in prison, of Dimmesdale's first hypocritical utterance before the people, and of the visit of Hester and Pearl to the Governor's mansion, where the minister's impassioned speech encourages the physician to undertake his "philosopher's research."

CHILLINGWORTH'S FORCE

In the second phase (Chapters 9–12), Chillingworth is the dominating force. Protected by Hester's vow of secrecy, he inflicts upon the minister a torture infinitely more diabolical than physical violence. Hawthorne's description of the process seems almost an anticipation of the psychiatric method: "So Roger Chillingworth—the man of skill, the kind and friendly physician—strove to go deep into his patient's bosom, delving among his principles, prying into his recollections, and probing everything with a cautious touch, like a treasure-seeker in a dark cavern. Few secrets can escape an investigator, who has opportunity and license to undertake such a quest, and skill to follow it up." But Chillingworth, unlike the modern psychiatrist, aims not to cure, but to torment; his motive is not scientific research, but revenge; he is changed, by degrees, from man to devil. Hawthorne describes his behavior upon discovering the scarlet letter (if such it was) on Dimmesdale's breast in language reminiscent of Milton's description of Satan: "With what a ghastly rapture . . . making itself even riotously manifest by the extravagant gestures with which he threw up his arms towards the ceiling, and stamped his foot upon the floor! Had a man seen old Roger Chillingworth at that moment of his ecstasy, he would have had no need to ask how Satan comports himself when a precious human soul is lost to heaven, and won into his kingdom." The second phase of the action ends with the complete subjection of the minister to Chillingworth: "He could play upon him as he chose." After the vigil on the scaffold, Dimmesdale yields to the physician's remonstrance and accompanies him to their habitat.

HESTER'S FORCE

Hester provides the counteraction of the third phase (Chapters 13–20). The minister's vigil has revealed to her his pitiable condition and made her conscious of the great wrong done him by her concealment of Chillingworth's true identity. She accordingly meets the minister in the forest, tells him that Chillingworth was her husband, implores and at length wins his forgiveness, urges upon him and secures his consent to their going away together. The effect of all this upon Dimmesdale is portrayed in the chapter "The Minister in a Maze": he experiences an unwonted vigor of body and mind; he resists, though with the greatest difficulty, a number of diabolical temptations as he passes through the town; and finally, having destroyed his old manuscript, he spends the rest of the night writing, like a man possessed, an entirely new Election Sermon.

DIMMESDALE'S FORCE

Thus energized, Dimmesdale determines the fourth phase, which is the remainder of the action, while Hester and Chillingworth lapse into secondary roles. It is important to note that Chillingworth's checkmating of the plan to escape, though known to Hester, is not known by Dimmesdale, and that while it serves the purpose of making Hester more amenable to the final outcome, it has no bearing on Dimmesdale's decision. The question may be fairly asked, perhaps, if the reader is properly prepared for the great confession, for it seems not entirely clear just when and how the minister's decision to confess came about. This is the only flaw—if it be such—in Hawthorne's entire design. At the end of Chapter 20, the author, it would seem, has deliberately withheld information necessary to a satisfactory preparation in order to accomplish the dramatic surprise of the confession scene. What has gone on in the minister's mind, however, can be plausibly surmised. After the alarming temptations that crowd him to the brink of self-betrayal, he is reduced to an unprecedented despair: "Am I mad?" he cries, "or am I given over utterly to the fiend?" Out of this struggle, greater than any that has preceded it, and out of this despair, comes a new, and now triumphant, reassertion of his better self. During the writing of the Election Sermon, it must be supposed, the minister, through divine grace, achieves for the first time a true repentance and, concomitantly, the will to confess.

Like the older, and unlike some of the more modern novelists (Henry James, for example), Hawthorne tells his story from a mixed point of view. He is sometimes an omniscient author, and sometimes an author of limited knowledge, professing ignorance of the true state of affairs. He is sometimes intrusive: he does not keep himself off the stage, as James was to insist on doing, but on occasion presents himself in the roles of historian and moral commentator. There are, however, in *The Scarlet Letter* long passages that anticipate the modern restricted point of view and, to a certain extent, the stream-of-consciousness. Some chapters are written largely from Chillingworth's point of view—e.g., "The Leech and His Patient"; others, from Hester's—e.g., "Pearl"; and still others, from Dimmesdale's—e.g., "The Minister in a Maze." This last, perhaps, is more completely confined to a single character than any of the others, and more nearly approaches the technique of James.

The changing point of view undoubtedly makes interpretation more difficult. The reader must distinguish among a variety of "authorities." Chillingworth is "kind and friendly" only in the sense that he consciously attempts to make himself appear so to the community. Pearl is portrayed, for the most part, as seen by Hester; the wild, ominous manifestations of her character are exaggerated by Hester's apprehensiveness. Hawthorne's method makes for ambiguity and uncertainty; the information at a given point must be appraised in relation to a shifting point of view.

THE SYMBOLICAL LANGUAGE

The book is frankly symbolical, and the author is constantly reaching out for larger meanings. The words "type" and "symbol" occur frequently. Hester is a "type of sin"; weeds growing on a grave "typify some hideous secret." The rosebush at the prison door "may symbolize some sweet moral blossom"; Pearl is "herself a symbol." Hawthorne's mind worked symbolically, and many explicit phrases like those just quoted compel a symbolical reading.

The action, therefore, is not to be taken too realistically, or subjected literal-mindedly to realistic tests. Many incidents, indeed, do violence to a literal realism. Chillingworth's physical deformity is symbolical of his spiritual depravity, and increases proportionately with his degradation, though in real life there need be no such correlation. In the forest scene, the

AN 1850 REVIEW OF *THE SCARLET LETTER*

On March 25, 1850, the Albany (New York) Daily State
Register *published a review of Nathaniel Hawthorne's* The
Scarlet Letter. *The reviewer praises Hawthorne as a writer
whose name on the title page of a new book brings pleasant
anticipation to readers because Hawthorne looks into the heart.*

There are some authors, the sight of whose name on the
title page of a new work comes with a freshness to our minds,
prophetic of the pleasure the perusal is to give us. Among
these is Hawthorne. Year after year we have taken up his
works, as they issued from the press, and always with unabat-
ed interest. His very style is a relief. It is an exception to the
exaggerated inflated verbiage of the day. Hawthorne writes in
the simple words of one who cares only to convey the ideas
with which his mind is so richly teeming. There is, too, about
his writings, an air of sympathy with mortal sorrow and
weakness. It is "the still sad music of humanity," and as we
read, we feel that we are following the lead of one, who has
obeyed [British poet] Sir Philip Sidney's rule,—"Look into thy
heart and write.". . .

But we must say nothing to forestall our readers as to the
conclusion. For although Hawthorne's works do not depend
for their interest upon the plot, and we are rather inclined to
linger on each page for the quiet beauty of the writing, yet still
it is better for the tale gradually to unfold before the reader,
and that it should not be anticipated by us.

"Literary Notices," *Albany Daily State Register,* 25 March 1850, 2:6, in *The
Critical Response to Nathaniel Hawthorne's* The Scarlet Letter, edited by Gary
Scharnhorst. Vol. 2, *Critical Responses in Arts and Letters.* New York: Greenwood
Press, 1992.

sunshine follows Pearl and avoids Hester; in the same scene, a
wolf approaches Pearl in friendly fashion. Such unrealistic
details symbolize Pearl's "natural" condition, her amenability
to nature's laws and to no others. Hawthorne called his long
fictions "romances." He claimed for them "a certain latitude,"
"a license with regard to every-day probability." The author of
a romance, he said [in the prefaces to *The House of the Seven
Gables* and *The Blithedale Romance*], "may so manage his
atmospherical medium as to bring out or mellow the lights
and deepen and enrich the shadows of the picture"; he may
also "mingle the Marvellous as a slight, delicate, and evanes-
cent flavor."

Hawthorne happily draws many of his symbols from the
beliefs and modes current in the time and place of his story;

by so doing, he achieves a superior integration and a certain historical validity. His chief symbol, the scarlet letter itself, is, as we have seen, a historical punishment. Imbedded, too, in early New England history is the belief in witchcraft, which is a fruitful source of symbols. The appearance during Dimmesdale's vigil of a meteor, in whose configuration the minister sees the letter *A*, is a skillful use of Puritan history. Hawthorne the historian gives an accurate account of the Puritan attitude toward extraordinary events in the natural world: "Nothing was more common, in those days," he says, "than to interpret all meteoric appearances, and other natural phenomena, that occurred with less regularity than the rise and set of sun and moon, as so many revelations from a supernatural source." Books like [Puritan teacher and intellectual] Increase Mather's *Remarkable Providences*, which Hawthorne knew well, confirm such a statement. "It was, indeed, a majestic idea," he adds, "that the destiny of nations should be revealed, in these awful hieroglyphics, on the cope of heaven." The general Puritan attitude is thus established. Dimmesdale agrees with this attitude when he looks for a divine message in the sky; but he stands in ironic contrast with the general attitude when he sees in the meteor a portent peculiar to himself. His reading of the heavenly symbol is a powerful and true expression of his morbid egotism and his isolation from the community.

Other symbols are so broad and natural that they are quite independent of any historical period; neither do they violate realism, or require a willing suspension of disbelief. An excellent example of this large class of symbols is the forest where Hester awaits Dimmesdale (and where, we may suppose, they had met as lovers, prior to the beginning of the story). This "primeval forest," we are told, "imaged not amiss the moral wilderness in which she had so long been wandering." It becomes, appropriately enough, the scene of another surrender to temptation. The symbol is a traditional one: [British poet] Edmund Spenser's characters in *The Faerie Queene* go astray in "Error's Wood."

It would be a mistake to assign fixed meanings to all of Hawthorne's symbols, for many of them are fluid and changing. Hester's *A* stands for adulteress; but to many in the community it comes to mean "Able." Pearl is an embodiment of the scarlet letter; her unnaturalness is seen as a reflection of her mother's guilty love. But in the forest scene she appears as a symbol of naturalness—the naturalness of nature itself. Chillingworth is pure intellect; but as the story progresses, he becomes the perversion and waste of intellect, and an incarnate devil, emitting fire. Dimmesdale stands chiefly for hypocrisy; at the end, he becomes its heroic opposite. Hawthorne's symbols—whether found in character, incident, or setting—are never rigid, but take on new meanings in the changing frame of reference.

THE HUMAN SITUATION

Hawthorne's aim in all of his fiction, he said, was to portray and reveal "the truth of the human heart." The persistent vitality of *The Scarlet Letter* would seem to be convincing evidence that in this, his greatest book, he succeeded in accomplishing his purpose. What are some of the facets of this truth of the human heart, as Hawthorne shows them in *The Scarlet Letter*?

The book abounds in the ironies, paradoxes, and ambiguities of human experience. It is ironical that Dimmesdale, who loves truth, should be a living lie; paradoxical that the deeper he sinks in falsehood, the more powerfully effective becomes his preaching of truth. It is ironical that Hester, who has such a large capacity for love, should be condemned to a loveless life; paradoxical that Pearl, the product of an unlawful union, should help Hester to keep the law; paradoxical and ironical that Chillingworth, the scientist, should pervert his science to human torture. Ambiguity, too, is everywhere in the story, for many questions do not admit of categorical answers. Hawthorne's language is repeatedly the language of ambiguity: "this might be pride, but was so like humility"; "it mattered little, for his object, whether celestial, or from what other region"; "the change may be for good or ill, and is partly, perhaps, for both"—are examples of ambiguous statement. Part of the wisdom of life consists in the recognition of the complexities and contradictions inherent in the human situation.

Hawthorne is seriously concerned in *The Scarlet Letter* with the difficulties involved in being human and with man's inhumanity to man. The passionate love of Hester and Arthur is extenuated: "What we did," Hester said to Arthur, "had a consecration of its own. We felt it so! We said so to each other!" The minister's hypocrisy is a pitiable thing, toward which one can be sympathetic, though mindful of the error, and from which he is happily saved in the end. But Chillingworth's sin is a crime beyond extenuation or redemption; it is what Hawthorne calls in another story ["Ethan Brand"], "the unpardonable sin." "That old man's revenge," says Dimmesdale, "has been blacker than my sin. He has violated, in cold blood, the sanctity of a human heart." It is no accident that Chillingworth is a scientist, though practicing a debased science in the story, for Hawthorne believed that the scientific mind, exclusively devoted to scientific pursuits, is peculiarly liable to the kind of dehumanization portrayed in Chillingworth.

Above all, Hawthorne is concerned in *The Scarlet Letter* with the problem of human isolation, the conditions of life that estrange man from, and those that unite him with, his fellow-men. The characters of the story are placed in false positions—false in relation to themselves, to each other, and to the community. This threefold falsity is seen in Chillingworth, in Dimmesdale, and in Hester. Chillingworth passes in the community for what he is not; he conceals from Dimmesdale and the world the fact that he is Hester's husband; he is false to his own scientific ideals. Dimmesdale, likewise, deceives the public; he is estranged from Chillingworth, Hester, and Pearl; he stultifies his own highest instinct—his love of spiritual truth. Hester's position, paradoxically, is the least difficult of the three: the great fact of her adultery stands mercifully revealed from the beginning. Since this is so, and since, unlike Dimmesdale, she does not regard their act as a violation of divine law, she is spared the kind of inner conflict that destroys the minister. Moreover, Pearl, though a punishment, is also a solace and support, and the open opposition of the community is conducive to the growth of fortitude. Hester is able and admirable; she is strong; and of the three characters, she is least estranged—therefore least unhappy—despite the ostracism of the scarlet letter. Her only deception in the story is her concealment from the minister of Chillingworth's identity. This one fault she corrects in the forest, in a scene of extraordinary power and tenderness.

Truth, in Hawthorne's view, is the one condition essential to happy human relations. "Among many morals," he says, "which press upon us from the poor minister's miserable experience, we put only this into a sentence: 'Be true ! Be true! Be true !'" Dimmesdale's lie is expunged by his public confession. By this act, and by his public recognition of Hester and Pearl as they stand together on the scaffold, he shows himself at last in a true light. He himself experiences an ineffable relief: "there was a sweet and gentle smile over his face, as of a spirit sinking into deep repose." More important, he establishes a true relation between himself and the two persons nearest him. The change in Pearl is symbolical of the new spiritual health achieved through sympathy.

Sin in Hawthorne may be defined as a violation or falsification of human relations. *The Scarlet Letter* is not about adultery as such, adultery being only a type or symbol of violation, or of any condition that leads to false relationships. Human connections, whether happy or unhappy, are inescapable, and when once established, they are, in a strict sense, indissoluble: the fixation of the characters in Boston is Hawthorne's allegorical way of saying this. A happy society cannot be achieved by law, by external management. There must be a magnetic chain, a true sympathy, joining individual persons together.

Hawthorne's treatment of all this is better than a tract would be. It is more moving, more profound, more enduring, for he has caught the whole human complexity in a memorable dramatic situation, and has embodied it in a work of remarkable restraint, unity, and intensity. The book, in short, becomes a living experience, which the reader can make his own.

CHRONOLOGY

1800

Thomas Jefferson elected president; reelected 1804.

1801

Hawthorne's parents, Nathaniel Hathorne and Elizabeth Manning, married on August 2.

1802

Hawthorne's sister Elizabeth born.

1803

United States buys Louisiana from France.

1804

Nathaniel Hawthorne born on July 4.

1804–1806

Lewis and Clark explore American Northwest.

1808

Captain Nathaniel Hathorne dies; Hawthorne's sister Maria Louisa born; James Madison elected president.

1809

Washington Irving publishes *Knickerbocker's History of New York*.

1812–1815

War with Great Britain.

1814

Francis Scott Key writes "The Star Spangled Banner"; Washington, D.C., burned by British troops.

1816

James Monroe elected president; Hathornes move to Maine.

1818

Hawthorne brought back to Salem to study.

1819–1820

Washington Irving publishes *The Sketch Book*.

1821

Hawthorne enters Bowdoin College.

1823

Monroe Doctrine proclaimed; James Fenimore Cooper begins *The Leatherstocking Tales.*

1825

Erie Canal opens; Hawthorne graduates from Bowdoin College.

1827

John James Audubon publishes *Birds of America.*

1828

Hawthorne publishes *Fanshawe*; Baltimore and Ohio Railroad establishes first passenger railroad in United States; Andrew Jackson elected president; Noah Webster publishes *An American Dictionary of the English Language.*

1830

Hawthorne publishes first tale in the *Salem Gazette.*

1831–1837

Hawthorne publishes twenty-two tales in the *Token.*

1833

American Anti-Slavery Society formed.

1835

Hawthorne publishes eight tales in the *New England Magazine.*

1836

Martin Van Buren elected president; Hawthorne edits the *American Magazine of Useful and Entertaining Knowledge*; Ralph Waldo Emerson publishes *Nature.*

1837

Hawthorne publishes *Twice-Told Tales.*

1838

Hawthorne becomes engaged to Sophia Peabody.

1839–1840

Hawthorne works at the Boston Custom House.

1841

Overland migration to California starts; Hawthorne publishes *Grandfather's Chair*; Hawthorne is a member of Brook Farm Community; President William Harrison dies and is succeeded by John Tyler.

1842

Hawthorne marries Sophia Peabody in Boston; newlyweds move to Old Manse.

1844

First message by Morse's telegraph; Edgar Allan Poe publishes "The Raven"; Hawthorne's daughter Una born.

1845

Texas annexed by United States; Hawthorne moves to Salem; Henry David Thoreau moves to Walden Pond.

1846

Elias Howe invents the sewing machine; Hawthorne's son, Julian, born; Hawthorne publishes *Mosses from an Old Manse*; begins work at the Salem Custom House.

1846–1848

War with Mexico.

1848

Women's Rights Convention at Seneca Falls, New York.

1848–1849

Gold discovered in California; gold rush begins.

1849

Hawthorne loses job at the Salem Custom House; mother, Elizabeth, dies.

1850

Hawthorne publishes *The Scarlet Letter*; moves family to Lenox, Massachusetts, where Hawthorne meets Herman Melville.

1851

New York Times established; Hawthorne's daughter Rose born; Hawthorne publishes *The House of the Seven Gables*; third edition of *Twice-Told Tales*; Hawthornes leave Lenox; Melville publishes *Moby-Dick*.

1852

Hawthorne publishes *The Blithedale Romance* and *A Wonder-Book for Girls and Boys*; Franklin Pierce, Hawthorne's friend, elected president; Harriet Beecher Stowe publishes *Uncle Tom's Cabin*; Hawthornes move to Wayside, in Concord, Massachusetts.

1853

Hawthorne's sister Maria Louisa killed in boat accident; Hawthorne publishes *Tanglewood Tales*.

1853–1857

Hawthorne serves as U.S. consul at Liverpool.

1854

Republican Party formed.

1855

Walt Whitman publishes *Leaves of Grass.*

1857

Supreme Court makes *Dred Scott* decision.

1857–1859

Hawthornes live in Italy.

1858

First stagecoach line from Missouri to Pacific coast established.

1859

John Brown raids Harpers Ferry; Hawthorne returns to England and finishes *The Marble Faun.*

1860

Pony Express runs from Missouri to California; Abraham Lincoln elected president; Hawthorne publishes *The Marble Faun*; Hawthornes return to America.

1861

Telegraph links east and west coasts.

1861–1865

American Civil War.

1862

First federal income tax; Lincoln issues Emancipation Proclamation; Julia Ward Howe publishes "The Battle Hymn of the Republic."

1863

Lincoln delivers Gettysburg Address; Hawthorne publishes *Our Old Home.*

1864

Lincoln reelected president; Hawthorne dies at Plymouth, New Hampshire, and is buried at Concord, Massachusetts.

1865

Lee surrenders at Appomattox; Lincoln assassinated and Andrew Johnson becomes president; Thirteenth Amendment abolishes slavery; Mark Twain publishes "The Celebrated Jumping Frog of Calaveras County."

WORKS BY HAWTHORNE

Nathaniel Hawthorne's works remain in print in a wide variety of anthologies and reissues; therefore, facts of publication are omitted from the following list.

1828

Fanshawe

1830

"The Hollow of Three Hills" published in the *Salem Gazette*

1831–1837

Twenty-two stories published in the *Token*

1837

Twice-Told Tales, first edition

1841

Grandfather's Chair
Famous Old People
Liberty Tree

1842

Twice-Told Tales, second edition
Biographical Stories for Children

1846

Mosses from an Old Manse

1850

The Scarlet Letter

1851

The House of the Seven Gables
Twice-Told Tales, third edition
The Snow Image and Other Twice-Told Tales

1852

A Wonder-Book for Girls and Boys
Life of Pierce
The Blithedale Romance

1853

Tanglewood Tales for Girls and Boys

1860

The Marble Faun

1863

Our Old Home

POSTHUMOUS PUBLICATIONS

1868

Passages from the American Notebooks

1870

Passages from the English Notebooks

1871

Passages from the French and Italian Notebooks

1872

Septimius Felton

1876

The Dolliver Romance

1883

Dr. Grimshawe's Secret
The Ancestral Footstep

FOR FURTHER RESEARCH

ABOUT NATHANIEL HAWTHORNE

Michael Davitt Bell, *Hawthorne and the Historical Romance of New England*. Princeton, NJ: Princeton University Press, 1971.

Millicent Bell, *Hawthorne's View of the Artist*. Albany: State University of New York, University Publishers, 1962.

W. C. Brownell, *American Prose Masters: Cooper-Hawthorne-Emerson-Poe-Lowell-Henry James*. Cambridge, MA: Belknap Press of Harvard University Press, 1967.

J. Donald Crowley, ed., *Nathaniel Hawthorne: A Collection of Criticism*. New York: McGraw-Hill, 1975.

Kenneth Dauber, *Rediscovering Hawthorne*. Princeton, NJ: Princeton University Press, 1977.

Neal Frank Doubleday, *Hawthorne's Early Tales: A Critical Study*. Durham, NC: Duke University Press, 1972.

Gloria C. Erlich, *Family Themes and Hawthorne's Fiction: The Tenacious Web*. New Brunswick, NJ: Rutgers University Press, 1984.

Richard Harter Fogle, *Hawthorne's Fiction: The Light and the Dark*. Norman: University of Oklahoma Press, 1964.

Nathaniel Hawthorne, *The American Notebooks*. Edited by Randall Stewart. New Haven, CT: Yale University Press, 1932.

Terence Martin, *Nathaniel Hawthorne*. Rev. ed. Twayne's United States Authors Series. Boston: Twayne Publishers, 1983.

Hugo McPherson, *Hawthorne as Myth-Maker: A Study in Imagination*. Toronto, Canada: University of Toronto Press, 1969.

Gary Scharnhorst, ed., *The Critical Response to Nathaniel Hawthorne's* The Scarlet Letter. Vol. 2, *Critical Responses in Arts and Letters*. New York: Greenwood Press, 1992.

Randall Stewart, *Nathaniel Hawthorne: A Biography*. New Haven, CT: Yale University Press, 1948.

Arlin Turner, *Nathaniel Hawthorne: An Introduction and Interpretation*. New York: Barnes and Noble, 1961.

Mark Van Doren, *Nathaniel Hawthorne*. New York: Viking, 1949.

Hyatt Howe Waggoner, *Hawthorne: A Critical Study*. Rev. ed. Cambridge, MA: Belknap Press of Harvard University Press, 1971.

———— , *Nathaniel Hawthorne*. University of Minnesota Pamphlets on American Writers, no. 23. Minneapolis: University of Minnesota Press, 1962.

HISTORICAL BACKGROUND FOR NEW ENGLAND

William Dudley and Teresa O'Neill, eds., *Puritanism: Opposing Viewpoints*. San Diego: Greenhaven Press, 1994.

Rod W. Horton and Herbert W. Edwards, *Background of American Literary Thought*. New York: Appleton-Century-Crofts, 1952.

Perry Miller, *The New England Mind: From Colony to Province*. Cambridge, MA: Harvard University Press, 1953.

———— , *The New England Mind: The Seventeenth Century*. Cambridge, MA: Harvard University Press, 1939.

Perry Miller and Thomas H. Johnson, eds., *The Puritans*. New York: Harper & Row, 1963.

Index